aloha stories

OUR PATH TO INNER AND GLOBAL PEACE

aloha stories

OUR PATH TO INNER AND GLOBAL PEACE

DR. CAROLE ALOHA HOPE LOCKARD

Aloha Stories: Our Path to Inner & Global Peace

http://www.AlohaStories.org

The author intends to offer information and her general insights to help the readers seek loving balance and harmonious well-being.

A portion of the proceeds from this book will be donated to the Aloha United Way, the American Red Cross, the Make-a-Wish Foundation, and the United Nations.

ISBN: 979-8-9887835-0-3 (paperback)
ISBN: 979-8-9887835-1-0 (eBook)

Library of Congress Control Number: 2023913169

Cover Artwork: Michael Bayouth
Cover Photos: Tomas del Amo
Editor: Pam Murphy

Other Works

Organizational Leadership Doctorate Degree Dissertation:
ALOHA STORIES
The Art of Storytelling Illustrating the Practice of Aloha
Dr. Carole Aloha Hope Lockard

Completed and Submitted November 2012

Carole wishes to gift you a complimentary PDF copy
of her Research Dissertation!
Your free copy is waiting for you at:
www.AlohaStories.org

Dedication

This book is a tribute to Pono Shim, an extraordinary Aloha Ambassador, mentor, and my spiritual big brother. I sincerely appreciate Pono for "seeing" and "prospering" (energetically lifting and celebrating) me throughout the years, starting with my dissertation research process.

Pono blessed me by generously sharing his gifts of wisdom related to his daily practice of *Aloha* (taught to him by his great aunt Pilahi Paki), along with his amazing storytelling and leadership insights.

May my *Aloha* involved in the creation of this book (as well as my Aloha Stories business efforts) continue to honor Pono's memory. I hope my efforts will also resonate with people, locally and globally, who are touched by this transformational, peaceful work.

Being forever thankful to Pono for encouraging me to be my unique self while absorbing the information he shared with me into my heart and soul (making it my own), I choose to continue my daily *Aloha* practice and share my *Aloha* stories with others through my perceptions, voice, as well as creative expressions.

A hui hou (until we meet again)… *Aloha*!

Table of Contents

Preface

My *Aloha* Story

Born and raised in a large, loving Portuguese family on the gorgeously lush windward side of the Hawaiian Island called Oahu, I experienced (and continue to witness) beauty everywhere. Surrounded by love manifesting in nature, people, animals, and experiences, I felt it was one glorious adventure… most of the time.

From my earliest childhood memories, I remember not fully understanding what people were saying, especially when there were many sounds around me, which was exacerbated when I felt either stressed or emotionally triggered, or both. In addition, numbers and letters danced (and continue to dance) in my head and on paper.

My verbal words at times flowed out of my mouth in mixed-up ways, not resembling the connected thoughts that were in my head. I believed everyone experienced life this way until I learned in preschool what it felt like to be labeled with hurtful words such as "Slow," "Stupid," and other demeaning labels. Back then, my parents, family, teachers, coaches, etc., did not have the awareness of neurological processing challenges that we do now.

From my first week in preschool throughout my elementary school years, my mother took me to multiple medical specialists to explore my vision, speech, and auditory challenges. Their findings were pretty much the same. My mother and I were told that my biological systems involved with my hearing, vision, and speech were fine, and I was just slow. I remember a few doctors saying that I might grow out of it and some of the doctors saying that I may remain that way for the rest of my life.

In reflection, I can now see that throughout my childhood and my young adulthood, I unconsciously overcompensated for what I did in life for attention and to prove to others that I was smart.

It is clear that my teaching gifts were born in my innate desire to help others learn, which evolved into a practice of "learning to teach," meaning mastering what I learned well enough to teach it to others. Consequently, I continue to thrive in academia and what I set my mind to because I've learned to integrate my superpowers of adaptive, intuitive, and creative abilities into my excelled study habits. This not only assisted me in assimilating information, systems, and processes but also transferred the gems from my learning experiences into unique, creative ways of educating others.

I love the Latin root meaning of "educate" *to bring out what is within.* One of my guided ways of helping others is in assisting them to see, feel, and know that the answers to what they seek to learn are already within themselves.

Being the eldest of six siblings and the oldest student in most of my classes (due to being born in December and held back a year in preschool), with the integration of nature and nurture, I evolved to be a leader in many arenas, including athletics, dancing, as well as drama (basically anything that was physical and involved storytelling, as well as creativity). My leadership instincts and the intuitive gifts that complemented my neurological challenges (such as being able to read people and energy) assisted me in being placed into leadership roles.

Being a natural servant leader with a strong desire to assist others who wanted help gifted me the opportunity to energetically lift, celebrate, and, at times, strategically protect myself along with others who bullies targeted.

When I was about seven years old, my hula teacher, Lorraine Brandt, introduced me to the values of *Aloha* (as developed by Pilahi Paki), which I flourished in like a fish in water. She also lifted my self-esteem by placing me in a teacher assistant (leadership) role, having noticed early on that I picked up the hulas effortlessly. I was quick to help the few classmates who were struggling in learning the hulas by teaching the hulas to them (while on the side of them) forwards, as well as (while facing them) backwards...mirror image. It felt good when Mrs. Brandt called me Miss *Aloha*, referring to the automatic helpful response I had for my classmates who needed extra assistance in learning the hulas.

Throughout my formative years, Mrs. Brandt (along with many of my sport and drama coaches) unintentionally assisted me in turning my neurological processing challenges into superpowers by encouraging me to focus my energy on my strengths, which complemented my interests rather than my weaknesses and mundane, repetitious memorization routines. These earthly angels fostered the *Aloha* spirit within me while nurturing my natural leadership abilities.

My parents enhanced my assimilation of *Aloha* through their daily life examples intertwined with their personal stories blended with stories about our earthly, along with heavenly original Portuguese (and evolving multi-cultural) family members.

It was a magical time for me, learning from compassionate family members the values of *Aloha*, witnessing their loving ways of being, and listening to their fascinating *Aloha* stories, which they enthusiastically shared with me. My parents continuously lifted and supported me with their love, especially when I was learning to navigate through sometimes painful bullying experiences.

In my mid-twenties, I was tested as a volunteer for neurological assessment tests at the relatively new Special Education Department at the University of Hawaii, Manoa campus. At the time, I was completing my Early Childhood and Elementary Education Teaching Certification Program after recently completing my undergraduate Biology degree at the College of Notre Dame, Belmont, CA.

The assessment team found that I exhibited high levels of auditory, visual, and speech dyslexia. These clinicians told me that there was little I could do to improve my condition because I was an adult, insinuating that I had passed the development window for significant healing and management of these neurologically-based challenges. I remember that their only suggestions were that I needed to accept my limitations and lower my expectations. Choosing not to accept these labels or their suggestions, I left the testing facility thinking their tests were flawed and they had much to learn.

Having mastered the art of hiding my processing challenges and making lemonade out of them the best I could (seeing the hidden gifts of my learning challenges as superpowers), I chose not to tell anyone about the tests and their results for many years. I also kept the test results to myself because I did not want the negative stigma that came with the test result labels. It wasn't until I had completed my Early Childhood and Elementary master's degree at Chaminade University in Hawaii (with additional Montessori certification) that I decided to finally share the findings of these assessments with my parents and family.

As I continued to teach early childhood and elementary classes in the following years, I shared my superpower learning tools (which I acquired along the way) with adults and children I was guided to assist. Choosing to shine a light on the students' strengths rather than their struggles, I found multi-sensory and open-ended learning projects in areas of their interest to be the most helpful ways of gifting many students (of various multi-intelligences) with loving, safe, and joyful integrative learning experiences. Throughout the years, this approach to learning helped many of my students, my daughter, and me to learn and heal harmoniously.

Feeling intuitively guided during my 20-plus years of teaching young children (and later the teachers of young children at the university level), I integrated age-appropriate curriculum to multi-sensory and multi-intelligence learning experiences with storytelling, as well as the values of *Aloha*, embedded in creative modalities (i.e., music, dance, sports, puppetry, videography, drama, art, in addition to authoring — to name a few). This glorious flow of multi-medium, multi-sensory, multi-intelligence storytelling experiences, incorporating *Aloha*'s values, lit the children and me on fire!

With *Aloha*, we shared our creative storytelling experiences with each other, starting with our one-to-one interactions and rippling out to our small group, class, and school uplifting experiences, which touched each of us and our families. The *Aloha* butterfly effect was in motion! The power of love and forgiveness (embedded in the *Aloha* values practice) was very contagious.

Many of my students shared similar life challenges with me and each other, which were rooted in our common human experiences, some of which included physical, emotional, family, financial, community, and sometimes learning difficulties. Channeling our energy via *Aloha* and sharing our evolving stories energetically elevated all involved, as it continues to do for me now… and will hopefully do so for you and your loved ones!

Fast forwarding to about thirteen years ago, I was gifted the opportunity to be a catalyst and a vessel of a once-in-a-lifetime research process, which not only met my requirements for my education doctorate degree in Organizational Leadership at Argosy University in Hawaii (distilling wisdom/information from education, business, and psychology arenas of study), but more importantly transformed me as a spiritual human being, and consequentially evolved my perspectives of life.

This unique research experience integrated my interests in *Aloha*, storytelling, and leadership. Pono Shim was an Aloha Ambassador, spiritual teacher, practitioner, Hawaii business leader, and an amazing storyteller whom I deeply respected.

Pono passed away in April of 2022. I am eternally grateful that Pono was divinely guided to be my mentor during the dissertation part of my journey. Pono was (and still is) my mentor and my spiritual big brother.

Pono's great aunt and mentor, Pilahi Paki shared with Pono the values of *Aloha* when he was a young boy. These were the same *Aloha* values my hula teacher, Lorraine Brandt, introduced me to and my parents/family members indirectly fostered in me from childhood to adulthood.

During one of my doctorate guest-speaking events, when I heard Pono speak about the *Aloha* values and storytelling the way his Aunty Pilahi taught him, I knew at a deep spiritual/energetic level that it was no accident to have been guided to hear Pono speak at that time.

A couple of months after my first experience hearing Pono speak, he graciously accepted my invitation to be the subject of my dissertation qualitative research case study, exploring the relationships between *Aloha,* storytelling, and leadership.

At the time of this case study, Pono Shim was an amazing Ambassador of Aloha, sharing his *Aloha* with his family, his community, and spiritually encompassing all the people of Hawaii... transformatively uplifting and celebrating "prospering" millions of lives. Pono graciously served as a board member for over 15 economic-related businesses in Hawaii. Being the Chief Executive Officer of Hawaii's Economic Board and Enterprise Honolulu, Pono worked daily with, consulted, and mentored many leaders in the Hawaiian Islands' business community.

It was my honor and privilege to be gifted the opportunity to be mentored by Pono during my dissertation process, as well as the years following this unique research experience. I encourage you to explore Pono's many interviews and resources online to gather more of a glimpse of this transformative Aloha Ambassador and teacher.

Growing up in the Hawaiian culture, my parents and family members imprinted the *Aloha* values and way of life on me by how they lived. Although I was not born with Hawaiian ancestry (Hawaiian blood), I always felt a strong-rooted connection to the Hawaiian Islands culture and people, embracing my understanding of the highly evolved universal *Aloha* values with my heart and soul.

Time and time again, Pono Shim reminded me that it did not matter if I had Hawaiian blood or not. He said what mattered was that I was practicing daily the universal *Aloha* values and sharing my stories evolving from my practice of *Aloha* with others when guided to do so.

Practicing the *Aloha* values daily, evolving into sharing my *Aloha* stories with others, is how I choose to be in this world and live my life. It resonates with who I am (love) and what I am here to do (to share love) in every spiritual, physical, and energetic aspect of my being.

With my *Aloha* stories sharing efforts here on earth, I hope that all people, locally and globally, who are touched by this noble work will embrace in their hearts (and practice in their daily lives) the values of

Aloha (love) expressed in their own unique voices, creative ways of being and *Aloha* stories, manifesting in our harmoniously transforming individual selves, our local communities and our global *ohana* (family).

I now choose to share this gift of *Aloha Stories* with you, individually and as a global community, highlighting my dissertation process in honor of Pono Shim. In addition, I choose to share with you my insights, experiences, and growth before, during, and after my doctorate-level research experiences. NOW, after going to that place of empty, feeling guided, with an open heart, lifting/prospering myself and others, I joyfully sing… *It is time*!

Acknowledgments

God/LOVE/Universe, I appreciate your gifts of eternal love and forgiveness in all that is in, through, and around me.

Mom (Antoinette "Toni" DeMello), Dad (Harold DeMello Jr.), and my other heavenly family angels, thank you very much for sharing your love, wisdom, and *Aloha* stories with me.

My earthly *ohana* (especially my husband, daughters, and five siblings), *mahalo* for your support, encouragement, and ever-abundant *Aloha.*

Heartfelt appreciation extends to my local and global communities, who have lovingly supported me during my journey, including friends, healers, counselors, mentors, coaches, and teachers.

Mahalo nui loa Pono Shim, Pilahi Paki, Alvin Shim, Morrnah Simeona, Lorraine Brandt, and Aunty Kaui (Kauihealani Mahikoa Brandt), for continuing to spiritually mentor and guide me with *Aloha.*

Pam Murphy, I appreciate your dedication, support, and guidance while you assisted me in birthing and launching this book.

Mahalo Michael Bayouth, thank you for creating my beautiful Aloha Stories business logo, book cover, and stunning promotional trailer.

Tomas del Amo, your generosity in donating the use of your gorgeous Hawaii photos for this book's back cover, trailer, and my Aloha Stories business is deeply appreciated.

Marci Shimoff, Dr. Sue Morter and my "Your Year of Miracles" *ohana*, thank you for your consistent love, support, and encouragement during this part of my life journey.

Thank you very much, Shelly Roby for your uplifting business coaching. You consistently encourage me to move through my fears and not be afraid to soar!

Eric Edmeades, you and your outstanding teams have been instrumental in my husband's and my transformation via your WildFit and Speaking Academy experiences. Thank you for sharing with us spiritually/energetically authentic, and biologically evolved ways of being.

Heart-felt appreciation is extended to Jean Houston and her dynamic team for mentoring me in the art/science of being fully human while "jumping time" and embracing transformational principles engulfed within quantum physics consciousness, as well as spirituality. Jean, you have helped me evolve in a way of being, fully soaring in my awareness of my entelechy (a realization of the vital source/force of my cosmic identity, and life/light purpose) I am LOVE! I am here to shine and share my love! Grazie!

To all of YOU readers, budding Aloha Ambassadors, and blooming Aloha Storytellers, thank you for your willingness to be open to this universally connecting language of *Aloha*, along with its evolved way of sharing *Aloha* via stories.

Lō kahi… we were, are, and forever will be connected…never broken. May we continue to be *Aloha* (love), as well as share our love via our *Aloha* stories in and through all that we are and do… "prospering" (lifting and celebrating) each other along the way.

Introduction

The secret to inner and global peace is being *Aloha* and sharing our *Aloha* stories.

Aloha means so much more than just hello or goodbye. *Aloha* means LOVE ~ a harmonious way of resonating at a higher frequency. It unites us via compassion, reverence, self-reflection, forgiveness, and patience. Through our daily practice of *Aloha*, our authentic *Aloha* stories evolve... and when shared with others, our *Aloha* stories connect, open, and heal us in transformative ways.

Aloha stories are interwoven with the deep-rooted wisdom of the Hawaiian culture to help us understand the life-changing ways all people can be *Aloha* ~ not just for themselves but for their families, their communities, and the entire world.

It all starts with an open heart, a willingness to embrace our shared humanity, and being vulnerable ~ coordinating mind, heart, and soul within each of us. Living *Aloha* and sharing our *Aloha* stories is our path to peace!

Let me be clear. I do not pretend to know all of life's answers, and I am far from perfect. Just like you, I am a learner during this life's journey. Feeling guided now, I choose to share the wisdom gems of my life experiences with you up until now, especially evolving from my research experiences with Pono Shim.

Not wishing to impose my spiritual beliefs on you, know that I choose to see all of us as co-leaders (co-creators) of our life journeys with or without a belief in a Higher Power (which I call God/LOVE/Universe), in addition to loving spiritual guides (which I call earthly and heavenly angels).

Being a co-leader/co-creator of my life journey, my curiosity about the integration of *Aloha*, storytelling (in all its delightful forms), and leadership (in relationship with self, family, and local/global/universal communities) fueled my work. My research, together with my life experiences, led me to my current transformative process of co-creating *Aloha Stories* that I now share with you. *Mahalo nui loa* (thank you very much) for following your guidance to *Aloha Stories*, which will hopefully assist all of us on our journey together.

With a heightened awareness of being vessels of *Aloha*, we have been, are, and continue to be subconsciously and, at times consciously co-creating our own *Aloha* stories. It is through these authentic *Aloha* stories that we internally and externally become aligned with our soul's life lessons, while mutually assisting other people with their life lessons.

My intention in this book, along with other aspects of my Aloha Stories business, is to share with you my *Aloha*, my ever-evolving *Aloha* stories, and my loving perspectives of life. The gems of wisdom Pono Shim and other Aloha Ambassadors have graciously shared with me are open-heartedly shared with you, as they were generously gifted to me.

I hope what resonates with you during our time together "prospers" (lifts and celebrates) you in your journey of discovery. May we feel connected via our common human experiences and inspired to practice the *Aloha* values daily, which evolves to sharing our *Aloha* stories with each other.

Here's what Pono encouraged me to do with what he taught me regarding *Aloha* and storytelling, and I now pass on to you. *Take it all in and make it your own. Then, share your perspectives and experiences related to your daily practice of Aloha with others in your own voice, style, and creative expression via your authentic Aloha stories.*

I learn best when I integrate as many traditional sensory mediums (i.e., sight, hearing, smell, taste, and touch) along with nontraditional sensorial mediums (i.e., emotional spectrums provoked in storytelling). Please make yourself comfortable and soak it all in via your unique ways of learning. Above all…enjoy the journey! Life is sweet!

My role as a guide on this *Aloha Stories* journey is intertwined with my roles as teacher and student. With your loving participation in this process, you are assisting me to learn some of my life lessons, as I am hopefully assisting you in learning a few of your life lessons.

A word of warning. Buckle up! At times, the road may be bumpy! It is meant to be that way. Our higher-level vibrations of being (reflected in our higher-level emotional states such as love, peace, gratitude, and joy) are at times more accessible when we consciously or unconsciously release our lower-level vibrations (reflected in our lower-level emotional states such as fear, anger, frustration, and jealousy) through forgiveness and other spiritual healing processes. Be patient with yourself and others!

These bumpy (sometimes painful) parts of our journey help us break open (spiritually, energetically, and emotionally) and release what needs to be shed to heal and grow. Know you are never alone and always well cared for by the God/LOVE/Universe and your spiritual guides. There is no right or wrong way to go about any of this. While loving yourself on this journey, sync your mind with your heart to align with your soul, take deep belly breaths filling yourself with (love, peace, and joy). Take a step forward (every second, minute, day, and year) to… keep beginning again with *Aloha.*

CHAPTER ONE

Beginning My Journey

♥♥♥

*"**Aloha**" connects people and all that exists!*

~ Pono Shim

Over thirteen years ago, I started my journey to discover how the practice of *Aloha* and the art of storytelling might enhance leadership and social responsibility to bridge the gaps between all people. I took a deep dive into the history and psychology of how the practice of *Aloha* reveals a sense of connection to all people.

Pilahi Paki and Alvin Shim created the Aloha Spirit Law in 1985. The Aloha Spirit Law introduces the five values of *Aloha* defined by Pilahi.

Aka hai means **kindness** to be expressed with **tenderness**

Lō kahi means **unity** to be expressed with **harmony**

Olu`olu means **agreeable** to be expressed with **pleasantness**

Ha`a ha`a means **humility** to be expressed with **modesty**

Aho nui means **patience** to be expressed with **perseverance**

Guides On My Journey

PILAHI PAKI

Pilahi Paki was Pono Shim's great aunt, known as "The Keeper of the Secrets of Hawaii." She was given the gift of '*ha*' (meaning the breath of life or the divine spirit) by Kaauana**luahine** Kaopua, known to Aunty Pilahi as Luahine and to the people of Hawaii as "the patriarch of Kona." On April 13, 1961, the gift of his '*ha*' (aka life wisdom) was given to Pilahi as Luahine transitioned in the Kona hospital.

As a gracious resource, Pilahi shared with all who wanted to learn the philosophy of Hawaii and the spirit of *Aloha*. She prophesized that in the 21st century, "The world will turn to Hawaii as they search for world peace because Hawaii has the key, and that key is *Aloha*."

Pilahi Paki was one of Hawaii's Living Treasures. She was related to Hawaii's Princess Bernice Pauahi's (Paki) Bishop and mentored many people currently leading the community of Hawaii.

ALVIN TONG SHIM

Throughout Alvin Shim's life, he consistently supported the little guy. From 1959 to 1962, as Chief Attorney for the Hawaii State House of Representatives, Alvin drafted bills resulting in key legislation that helped generations of people in the Hawaiian Islands. One of his most groundbreaking efforts was to ensure a health care and retirement system for Hawaii's government employees, which would later become a model for the United States. In 1973, Alvin was the significant force in drafting and passing Hawaii's No-Fault Insurance Law.

Alvin believed in and supported the education and empowerment of Hawaiians, particularly the mission of Kamehameha Schools. In 1975, he co-founded Alu Like, Inc., and in 1978, he planted the seed to establish the Office of Hawaiian Affairs.

With Pilahi Paki's help in 1985, Alvin created the Aloha Spirit Law. In 1986, Alvin lobbied to have the "Aloha Spirit" concept written into state law so that all citizens would conduct themselves in accordance with this law. He understood Hawaii's social fabric and believed in every human being's inherent good nature, which manifested in Alvin actively seeking ways to improve the human condition. He not only made a difference in shaping and improving the quality of life for many people in Hawaii, but he also touched their hearts and souls. Alvin inspired all those he encountered to think deeper, love stronger, and fully live every moment.

PONO SHIM

Pono was the son of Alvin Shim and was, in his own right, a recognized business leader in the Oahu, Hawaii community. At the time I met Pono, he was participating as a board member for about 15 economic-related businesses on Oahu. Being the Chief Executive Officer of Hawaii's Economic Board and Enterprise Honolulu, he worked with, consulted, and mentored many leaders in the business community. Pono passed away on April 8, 2022.

In Pono's own words, he shares his experience when Aunty Pilahi told him she was going to teach him.

"The year was 1976. Hokulea had searched for and found Tahiti and, at the same time, launched selected individuals on a lifetime journey to recover lost knowledge. As they recovered and discovered the knowledge that allowed our Hawaiian ancestors to transmigrate across the earth's most expansive ocean, they became a resource for the world, and in so doing, their effectual impact was far greater than the knowledge they carried as celestial navigators.

And equally important, they became living examples of deep Hawaiian values. At that moment, I was a 13-year-old boy tagging along with my father to a meeting with Aunty Pilahi (Paki) and other (mostly) Hawaiian leaders.

Aunty Pilahi sat facing everyone else, and I sat in the back of the room in an elevated area that allowed me to see everything. There was a lot of emotion and heartache in this meeting. Topics included Kahoolawe, Kalama Valley, Waiahole water rights, Sand Island evictions, Ceded lands, Annexation and Statehood, and the overthrow of our kingdom. I remember thinking to myself, *These are really angry people.*

Aunty Pilahi was very gentle as she listened, and she would respond with stories or illustrations that seemed to **disarm** people and **calm** the room down. The room would be calm for a little while, and then it would erupt again in a different conversation, and she would **shift the energy** again. I watched this for about 4 hours, and then she concluded and waited for almost everyone to depart.

She walked up to me and asked me to walk with her. When we were alone, she said, 'Pono, I'm going to teach you to practice. I'm going to teach you the deeper meanings of some words and how to practice them in relationships. **I want you to learn how to think Hawaiian**, not speak Hawaiian. I want you to know Hawaiian thought. If you think Hawaiian, regardless of the language you use, it will be the language of *Aloha,* and *Aloha* is the language that reveals the connection to all people.'

Aunty Pilahi then shared this 1917 quote from Queen Liliuokalani and directed me to the last line. She said, 'Most people interpret the last line to mean that on earth, there is man and woman and in heaven, there is God. But there's a hidden message, and with Hawaiian thought, you can find the message.

> I could not turn back the time for the political change, but there is still time to save our heritage. You must remember to never cease to act because you fear to fail. The way to lose an earthly kingdom is to be inflexible, intolerant, and prejudicial. Another way is to be too flexible, tolerant of too many wrongs and without judgment at all. It is a razor's edge. ***It is the width of a blade of pili grass***. To gain the kingdom of heaven is to hear what is not said, to see what cannot be seen, and to know the unknowable — that is *Aloha.* All things in this world are two, in heaven there is but one.

The message is that on earth, there are always at least two sides to a story, but in heaven, there's only one story that includes all sides.'

'Pono,' she said, 'you will become a storyteller, but you will tell the stories in the old ways, the stories of connections. When you tell your stories, you must practice telling them from heaven's perspective.'"

Moving On

It has been suggested that the values of *Aloha* come from the Hawaiian people and the Hawaiian culture. The people of Hawaii have invested in the notion that the *Aloha* values are part of their culture.

I intended to dig into what designated *Aloha* and its inherent values as being universal and a part of everyone's evolutionary process of becoming a whole multi-sensory human being. I explored the possibility of *Aloha* being the unifying language that can be used for human evolution to enhance connectedness and appreciation of the collective human noble spirit.

One of my goals was to learn to use storytelling as a tool to assimilate and integrate, as Aunty Pilahi described it to Pono Shim, "...to learn how to think Hawaiian.

During the dissertation process, Pono invited me not to try so hard to understand with my head what he was teaching me but rather shift my energy to intuitively absorbing with my heart and soul the deeper universal, energetic, and spiritually human experience-based expressions along with connections of *Aloha*, which he (and Pilahi Paki) called the *Aloha* values.

Originally, I thought the values of the Hawaiian culture resulted in the values of *Aloha*. Through an exploration of the literature and my case study of Pono Shim, I found a connection between the importance of the universal values of *Aloha* and storytelling as they pertain to local and global leadership and social responsibility. These connections excited me because they resonated with what I intuitively knew to be true!

Various cultures worldwide emulate social responsibility in ways based on their values. These values are shaped by perceptions of relationships with self, a possible Higher Power, the Universe, people of other cultures, and nature. Many cultures taught and continue to teach socially responsible values through the art of storytelling. The Hawaiian culture continues to teach *kuleana* (responsibility) through a way of being called *Aloha*, which emulates from hula, music, art, and storytelling.

Aloha is most commonly associated with the Hawaiian word for love and the hospitable customs of greeting and wishing loved ones farewell. Breaking down the parts of Hawaiian words provides a deeper awareness and appreciation of their meanings. The Hawaiian meaning of '*alo*' means to be face-to-face and in the presence of another. '*Ha*' means the breath of life or the divine spirit, as well as life wisdom. When combined, *Aloha* is the presence of the divine spirit in each other.

The ancient spiritual *Aloha* practice of greeting along with farewell of the Hawaiian people is shared with other indigenous cultures such as the native people of America, Samoa, Mari, and Alaska. It is generally expressed by two people gently placing their foreheads and noses together, inhaling and exhaling, and simultaneously sharing their breath. The universal importance of '*alo*' (i.e., face-to-face presence) and '*ha*' (i.e., sharing of breath) is one of the deeper universal spirituals and physical human experiences based on *Aloha* expressions.

There seems to be a similarity of the meaning of the Sanskrit word *namaste* to the meaning of *Aloha*, suggesting that the unifying concepts of the divine spirit present in oneself, as well as other people, were deeper meanings of both words, *namaste* and *Aloha*.

The essence of *namaste* has been described as the awareness of the light or Creator (love) in one person recognizing the light or Creator (love) in the other person. The description of *Aloha* can be paralleled with the meaning of *namaste* by suggesting *Aloha* was a way of being that allowed each person's humanness and Creator (love) to be recognized and honored by other spiritual (love) human beings.

In my research, I searched for the meaning of *Aloha* through the art of storytelling pertaining to human evolution expressed in an inclusive and compassionate postmodern lens manifesting in global social responsibility enhancing individual self-reflected leadership.

I explored what can be understood about leadership as it emanates from the practice of *Aloha* on Oahu. My research and study about leadership along with *Aloha* developed through an investigation of the art of storytelling by interviewing plus observing a storyteller, Pono Shim, who also happened to be a recognized Ambassador of Aloha and a business leader in the Oahu community.

As I delved more into my research, I became more and more enthralled to learn through Pono Shim how the practice of *Aloha* complementing the art of storytelling helped create social responsibility in leadership. Pono was a treasure trove of information as I explored his espoused and practiced theories of the art of storytelling, illustrating the practice of *Aloha*.

One of the many challenges I faced was translating all the subtle meanings of *Aloha* and the Hawaiian cultural perspective of leadership and social responsibility that are sometimes lost in the movement from one language to another. To understand the Hawaiian thought based in the Hawaiian culture is to truly understand the meanings and intentions of the words used to describe *Aloha's* core concepts.

Pono suggested in his interviews and my observations that *Aloha* is universal. He clarified that an understanding of *Aloha* can be deepened with an understanding and experience of the human condition, not just the Hawaiian culture.

I participated in storytelling and *Aloha* workshops facilitated by Pono that were sponsored by Argosy University Hawaii campus, in addition to Enterprise Honolulu prior to the beginning of my research dissertation process, leading to some bias in the form of preconceived ideas about storytelling and *Aloha*. I did my best to let go of what needed to be released related to my preconceived ideas to be open-minded before each of Pono's interviews, along with my observations.

My desire to be *Aloha* and practice the art of storytelling while studying the concepts related to *Aloha* and storytelling was my underlying attempt to understand the two integrated phenomena fully. My research study described the concept of the art of storytelling, illustrating the practice of *Aloha* integrating Pono Shim's perspectives.

The significance of this concept begins the discussion of how the universal along with the humanistic values of *Aloha* can be communicated using the visual, kinesthetic, and audible intelligence rich medium of storytelling with the intuitive, spiritual, multiintelligence, sensory, and ultra-sensory language of *Aloha,* enhancing an evolved concept of interconnectedness resulting in global harmonious unity.

Born and raised on the island of Oahu, living most of my life immersed in the multicultural influences that are a part of Hawaii, I was intrigued with the universal values of *Aloha,* along with its possible influence on individual and global leadership evolving into world peace.

In observing, witnessing, and experiencing the concepts surrounding the values of *Aloha* related to the study of storytelling, I intended not only to study the concepts with my mind but also to immerse myself (heart, body, mind, and soul) into the process. Pono invited me to "practice *Aloha*" and the art of storytelling as he presented them during my research experience.

CHAPTER TWO

Let's Get Started!

♥♥♥

"Aloha" is to hear what is not said,
to see what cannot be seen,
and know the unknowable!

~ Pilahi Paki

Before diving deeper into *Aloha Stories*, this chapter gives you the foundational tools to develop and deepen your perspective. *Aloha*, storytelling, social responsibility mingled with spirituality, and co-creation in leadership are interconnected. These concepts can be fully understood and experienced.

The Definition of *Aloha*

Experiencing *Aloha*, as Pilahi Paki describes, is to hear what is not said, see what cannot be seen, and know the unknowable. *Aloha* includes mutual regard and affection, as well as an extension of warmth in caring with no obligation. It's the essence of relationships in which each person is important to every other person in a collective existence.

Aunty Pilahi's definition of *Aloha* and description of its values (embedded in the *ALOHA* acronym) introduces *Aloha* as a way of life that connects people and everything that exists. To illustrate its fullness, Pilahi defined *Aloha* from several different perspectives. These definitions, when blended, create a beautiful harmony unified in one magnificent sound. Alvin Shim and Pilahi Paki expanded the description of the philosophy and values of *Aloha* in the Aloha Spirit Law, including the *Aloha* philosophy and values.

The Aloha Spirit Law

The Aloha Spirit Law is an ACTUAL law "on the books" in Hawaii, encoded in the Hawaii Revised Statutes, §5-7.5, and acknowledges that The Aloha Spirit "was the working philosophy of native Hawaiians and was presented as a gift to the people of Hawaii."

The law states: All citizens and government officials of Hawaii are obligated by law to conduct themselves in accordance with this law, while performing their duties and obligations, as well as in their day-to-day living. Likewise, those visiting our fair islands are expected to conduct themselves in accordance with this Hawaiian law.

The Aloha Spirit elevates, empowers, and ennobles its people, and KEEPS Hawaii the uniquely special place that it is. The Aloha Spirit Law deserves our unmitigated support and compliance. As a model law for the world, it can serve the greatest number for its greatest good.

Together, we can make the Aloha Spirit as vibrant and REAL as it was for those who came before us. Those who have experienced The Aloha Spirit have an obligation to make it real for those who follow. An individual, conscious effort is required. Let it begin with me and you.

Full Test of THE ALOHA SPIRIT LAW

§5-7.5 The Aloha Spirit.

(a) "Aloha Spirit" is the coordination of mind and heart within each person. It brings each person to the Self. Each person must think and emote good feelings to others. In the contemplation and presence of the life force, "Aloha," the following *unuhi laula loa* (free translation) may be used:

Aka hai, meaning kindness, to be expressed with tenderness;
Lō kahi, meaning unity, to be expressed with harmony;
Olu`olu, meaning agreeable, to be expressed with pleasantness;
Ha`a ha`a, meaning humility, to be expressed with modesty;
Aho nui, meaning patience, to be expressed with perseverance.

These are traits of character that express the charm, warmth, and sincerity of Hawaii's people. It was the working philosophy of native Hawaiians and was presented as a gift to the people of Hawaii. "Aloha" is more than a word of greeting or farewell or a salutation. "Aloha" means mutual regard and affection and extends warmth in caring with no obligation. "Aloha" is the essence of relationships in which each person is essential to every other person for collective existence. "Aloha" means to hear what is not said, to see what cannot be seen and to know the unknowable.

(b) In exercising their power on behalf of the people and in fulfillment of their responsibilities, obligations and service to the people, the legislature, governor, lieutenant governor, executive officers of each department, the chief justice, associate justices, and judges of the appellate, circuit, and district courts may contemplate and reside with the life force and give consideration to the "Aloha Spirit."

Alvin declared: "To the Hawaii of Old, "The Spirit of Aloha" was a concept REAL and vital to the existence of her people. "Aloha" was the spiritual essence of life. "Aloha" was a philosophy, a way of living, a code in life. The "Aloha Spirit" Law defines and expresses the characteristics and traits of that Spirit. These words were not composed by but conveyed to Pilahi Paki, a *makua* (parent/elder) with a purpose and responsibility, a *kulean*a. That *kuleana* was to carry and pass on the message of Aloha."

Alvin then added: "Do not neglect to show hospitality to strangers, for by doing that, some have entertained angels unaware" and "*O ke aloha ke kuleana o kâhi malihini*" ~ "Love is the host of strange places."

In old Hawaii, every passerby, whether a total stranger or acquaintance, was greeted and offered hospitality. Aunty Pilahi Paki invited each person to contemplate and practice the working philosophy of the native Hawaiians expressed in *Aloha*, coordinating the mind and heart of each individual to bring each person to self. She even suggested that the practice of *Aloha* resulted in relationships built on mutual regard and affection.

If global and multicultural leaders embrace and teach social responsibility through *Aloha*, the world's transition from modernism (i.e., centered on exclusivity and competitiveness) to postmodernism (i.e., centered on collaboration, connection, cooperation, and inclusivity) would be enhanced.

Aloha has also been defined as unconditional love, which includes the universal values of cooperation, caring, and generosity inherent in the philosophy and practice of *Aloha* that may enable global leaders to create a prosperous future for generations to come.

Raising the awareness of multicultural and global leaders related to the already existing humanitarian and socially responsible universal values emulated in *Aloha* through storytelling will help move the global *ohana* (family) toward world peace. This enhanced transition from modernism to postmodernism, through the practice of *Aloha* evolved from storytelling, will enable global leaders to create a prosperous future for all humans.

Pilahi Paki is revered as one of Hawaii's Ambassadors of Aloha who embodied the spirit of *Aloha*. Aunty Pilahi illustrated, through the art of storytelling, the components of *Aloha* and taught the art of storytelling to her students, including Pono Shim. Even today, the components of *Aloha* continue to be taught through the art of storytelling.

Pilahi Paki and Alvin Shim clarified that the values of *Aloha* are not just Hawaiian; they are universal values that resonate with every culture on earth. Social responsibility in the leadership of multicultural leaders complements these universal values of *Aloha*. Pono Shim reiterated Aunty Pilahi's belief that *Aloha* invites each person to coordinate their mind and heart to bring each person to self, resulting in relationships built on mutual regard, reflected in feelings of affection.

Again, the Aloha Spirit Law invites each person to contemplate and practice the working philosophy of the native Hawaiians expressed in *Aloha*. The Aloha Spirit Law was legally approved after Aunty Pilahi's passing in 1986.

Storytelling

My research and experiences showed me that the use of language is not straightforward because familiar words do not carry identical meanings. These words only elicit meanings that already exist in your brain. The meaning of familiar words depends on your relevant physical and emotional experiences and the context in which the words are used. This illustrates the need for a universal language to create unity via shared experiences and emotions, as demonstrated in the practice of *Aloha,* along with storytelling.

This is important and bears repeating. Stories are made up of words. The listener's perceptions and understood meanings of the words depend on that individual's physical and emotional experiences!

In other words, your experiences define your specific definition or expectation of each word's meaning. Therefore, two people, each with unique experiences, frequently define words differently.

When two or more people acquire the same meanings for words and knowledge of the same guidelines for combining the words to express meaning (i.e., syntax), this mutual language results in the use of words to transmit common meaning from one person to another.

In many cultures, storytelling transfers wisdom from one generation to the next via shared common human experiences. In the Hawaiian culture, the art of storytelling has been woven with the practice of *Aloha*.

When Pono Shim was a boy, his great aunt Pilahi Paki asked him to walk with her after observing a meeting of mainly Hawaiian people. During this walk, Pilahi shared with Pono the values of *Aloha* and a vision to be a storyteller in a unique way.

Pilahi Paki instructed Pono to be a storyteller by telling stories in the old ways of connections and integrating the *Aloha* values. Pilahi continued by teaching Pono how to tell stories from heaven's perspective, including all sides.

Over the years, Pilahi taught Pono how to think Hawaiian, not speak Hawaiian. To think Hawaiian meant to be sensitive to the human experience from an elevated perspective. Pilahi shared with Pono her perspectives of the values of *Aloha* and told Pono to practice.

In my research, I realized that stories are how people remember. That narrative imagining — or story — is the fundamental vehicle of thought. Stories are humans' chief means of looking into the future, planning, predicting, and explaining. Most human experience, knowledge base, and thinking process can be organized as stories. Human beings are wired to understand stories, not logic.

Story is present where high concept and high touch intersect. A story is considered as *high concept* due to its ability to sharpen understanding of one thing by showing it in the context of something else.

A story is *high touch* because of its ability to evoke emotion. Stories also have the good capacity to capture exactly those elements that formal decision methods leave out. Stories capture the context and capture the emotions. In essence, stories are more important than logical events because they encapsulate into one compact package: information, knowledge, context, and emotion.

The meaning provided by stories and storytelling about the storyteller's experiences relatable to the audience's human and emotional experiences is the key to helping humans connect and uncover meaning in their lives. To summarize and simplify, to give context and idealize are key abilities of stories and storytelling, which are important in the current Conceptual Age and human evolution. Becoming skilled at the ability to place facts into context and deliver them with emotional impact in relatable stories is crucial to human evolution.

It has been argued that the "hero's journey" has been the blueprint for tales since the beginning of time and includes three main parts: departure, initiation, and return. In other words, the hero hears a calling, initially refuses the calling, and then crosses over to the threshold into a new world, which is the departure portion. During the initiation part of the journey, the hero faces difficult challenges and stares into the abyss. While in the initiation phase of the journey, with the help of a mentor, the hero is given a divine gift that transforms and enables the hero to be at one with him or herself.

The journey of the hero ends with a homecoming, where the hero returns as the master of two worlds, committed to improving each of the two worlds. This hero's journey structure in stories and storytelling can be found in epic tales such as Homer's *Odyssey,* the legend of King Arthur, *Huckleberry Finn,* the story of Buddha, the story of Sacagawea, *Star Wars, Pandora,* and *The Matrix.* The human experience is that of challenge, exploration, and discovery.

Storytelling is the narrative way humans share their experiences to connect with each person emotionally, spiritually, and sensorially. Human beings' tendencies to explain their perceptions of their world in narrative stories are so deep and ingrained that we are often not even aware of it. This deep-rooted, innate drive to share our personal stories of life wisdom with others has been dormant during the past few ages and must be re-awakened during the current Conceptual Age.

Social Responsibility Integrated with Spirituality in Leadership

Social responsibility combined with spirituality in multicultural leadership complements *Aloha*'s universal values. Mahatma Gandhi and Margaret Wheatley were major thought leaders in social responsibility and spirituality in leadership. Gandhi and Wheatley provided the foundation for my exploration of the phenomenon of social responsibility and spirituality exhibited by leaders in various cultures around the world.

Common contributions that complement the *Aloha* values include:

- ***Self-reflection***, present in the practice of Ha`a ha`a and Aho nui
- ***Unity***, present in the practice of Lō kahi
- **Humility** and **compassion**, present in the practice of Aka hai and Olu`olu

Self-Reflection

Leaders such as Gandhi created a ripple effect by inspiring people to be the change they wished to see in their world, initiated through self-reflection. As a quiet leader, Gandhi led by example, symbolically walking to the ocean to get salt for his food and fostering peace by being peaceful in his daily choices. This example of leadership is a reflective aspect of social responsibility, where a cooling and quieting process enhances a leader's innate curiosity and patience before taking action.

Multicultural leaders can be transparent by accepting weaknesses and awareness of fear-generated triggers from their daily practice of self-reflection. It has been noted that leaders such as Gandhi are able to remember who they are and unveil their life purpose through mindfulness, meditation, and self-reflection.

In practicing mindfulness, meditation, and self-reflection, these leaders catalyze and galvanize a ripple effect of awakened awareness of their life purposes and the people they serve.

It has also been pointed out that a leader's strengths, weaknesses, fears, and motivations are unveiled through this deep exploration of self via self-reflection. Once this process starts with the leader and the team members, trust and caring of team members can begin to grow.

Leaders must live self-examined lives and fulfill Socrates' proclamation that an unexamined life is not worth living. Gandhi's ability to reflect before initiating socially responsible acts was rooted in his awareness of self, created from meditation and reflection. Reflective, quiet leaders "think about doing the right thing in a different way."

It is in the practice of taking time to reflect that leaders internally explore their bias and inner conflict, which sheds light on the larger challenges of the organization. Through being aware of self, bias, and the larger picture, leaders can be empowered to operate at a higher frequency, make choices that creatively navigate within the limits of the organization's fear-based policies, and transcend fear to honor each noble spirit.

In self-reflection, leaders allow themselves to explore bias, triggers, and unresolved family of origin or relationship issues in an effort to clean their internal house before action.

Through self-reflection, leaders also gift themselves the space and time to step back from daily challenges and wonder about creative solutions. Self-reflection and mindfulness are the core of empowerment and socially responsible leadership. When the leader practices mindfulness and self-reflection, the effects of these practices ripple throughout the community.

Unity

Gandhi was deeply aware of the human condition and connectedness to each other and to nature. It was through Gandhi's ability to simplify his life, to be vulnerable, and to be in the moment that he opened himself up to the unifying song of humanity.

Leaders capable of being vulnerable, standing transparent, and exposing their human weaknesses to their team members are deeply aware of the connectedness of being human. Through a leader's vigilant creation of a safe environment that is free of competition, this unity awareness can be fostered.

The dynamics of relationships and the ability to create an authentic awareness of unity are more important than required tasks, functions, roles, and positions within the company. People in organizations are unwilling to take action, make changes, or make decisions until trust and inclusion are established and they feel heard and appreciated.

An organization's power and energy are generated by strengthening personal relationships by building trust from sharing human vulnerability that unifies rather than separates members in the community.

It has been noted that by taking the time to hear the stories and getting to know team members, leaders discover their similarities and, therefore, catalyze innate unity that binds organizations together. Also, through listening to and observing team members, leaders become aware of the hidden talents, weaknesses, hopes, dreams, and struggles of fellow organizational members. Leaders are encouraged to develop skills in themselves and support the development of skills in their team members to enhance unity by embracing listening along with the awareness of the needs of team members.

Leaders can create unity by taking the time to swap stories via casual visits, "talking story" with their fellow team members to get to know their team, for team members to get to know their leaders, and for all involved to get a sense of each other's needs, wants and dreams. It is through a leader's effort of co-creating an environment rich with a feeling of shared humanity that a team's connectedness truly becomes apparent.

This exchange of stories can reveal what innately motivates team members, team leaders, as well as what generates fear that blocks or demobilizes all team members of the organization. It is extremely important that people take the time not just to listen with their ears but also to truly hear with their hearts the stories of fellow team members.

A new paradigm has been discovered that humanity's potential is a fully conscious super organism in an awakening universe through the alignment with the ancient concept of Gaia (or Earth) being a living organism in which every human being is a cell in the planetary nervous system.

Breakthroughs in telecommunication and computer networks are connecting the human species to an embryonic global brain. This rapid rate of connectivity, especially with the current explosive growth spurt of AI (artificial intelligence) integrating into our daily lives, is affecting business, politics, medicine, and all aspects of life on Earth and within our universe. This includes our evolving relationship perspectives about ourselves internally/externally, locally/globally, and microcosm/macrocosm.

In fact, the current evolutionary shift in consciousness is moving from egocentrism to geo-centrism. A unifying language connecting all of humanity parallels the unifying language of *Aloha* as described by Aunty Pilahi Paki in her synthesis of *Aloha* values.

Humility and Compassion

Through the awareness of human connectivity, leaders seek more information, including insights into personal and global conflicts and challenges, thereby demonstrating humility. Knowing the whole story is the core of humility. Humility is defined as a brave, rare act in which an individual admits that they do not have the answer.

It has been concluded that humility is impossible in communities built on competition. Communities that value and practice inclusion-enhancing collaboration experience humility, connection, and compassion for their team members and those outside their community.

Compassion refers to acknowledging humanity and recognizing that no person truly knows the whole story. Through embracing their damaged selves and members of their communities, humans develop grace and compassion. Some describe compassion as permission to sit on the same side of the table and have the problem sit on the opposite side.

When leaders lead with compassion, they understand that being human means everyone is limited by the inability to see the big picture; therefore, humans are united in their ignorance. Through storytelling, the awareness of human innocence and ignorance is shared, resulting in shared compassion and humility.

Gandhi exemplified humility by recognizing that he could not fully understand the whole story of the core issues that caused his people in India to suffer. It was humbling for him, being highly educated and a lawyer, to admit that he did not have the answers to the problems of his people.

It has been suggested that compassion touched Gandhi's heart and rippled through the hearts of the people in India when Gandhi demonstrated peacefully, making it clear that he was aware that his people did not understand the whole story either. Gandhi did not know the complete answer to the problem of injustice and suffering experienced by the people of India; however, Gandhi did know that peace, along with non-violent actions, was part of the solution. He chose to be peaceful and radiate that peaceful energy among his community.

Gandhi's peaceful way of being inspired others to be peaceful in their words and actions. Gandhi not only empathized with and felt the pain of his people, but he also demonstrated humility and compassion in a peaceful and non-violent manner to bring about the result he wished to see in himself, his community, and the world.

Gandhi explained that the first step in non-violence is for human beings to cultivate peace in their daily life practices with self along with others and to display truthfulness, humility, tolerance, and loving kindness. In the principles of *Aloha*, being humble is where social responsibility begins. To be humble is to be aware of one's humanity and that the opposite of being humble is to expect perfection from others and oneself. This mindset of perfection leads to competition, destruction, and war.

Social responsibility does not evolve out of the rhetoric of a company's declaration of socially responsible projects but rather from the caring actions of individuals within the organization for each other, their families, and members of other organizations. By expressing the full spectrum of human emotions, leaders develop a state of artfulness recognizing the wondrous qualities of the human being. It is through this state (i.e., awareness and expression) of emotional sensitivity enhanced by empathy that caring action stems from humility and compassion. This heightened emotional state has been described as a form of emotional intelligence.

Many have and still advocate leadership with a heightened awareness of unity, social responsibility, humility, compassion, and spirituality in our evolving world. Gandhi's original intent of being self-efficient grew to encompass a leader's social responsibility and spirituality at its highest level. Throughout history, leaders and societies of various evolved cultures have exemplified heightened awareness of social responsibility and spirituality, illustrating the connectedness of a species, which assisted them in transitioning through uncertain times.

Social responsibility and spirituality are intertwined in leaders of various cultures. Research unveiled a glimpse of the spirit of social responsibility and spirituality in leadership through the exploration of self-reflection, unity, humility, and compassion. These universal values of global leaders complement the universal values of *Aloha*.

History of Postmodernism that Developed from Modernism

In the realm of sociology, Louis Hoffman summarized that the evolution of humans has been described (in terms of periods of time and dominant philosophies) in three arenas: premodernism (up to 1650s), modernism (1650s to 1950s), and postmodernism (1950s to current times).

When exploring these terms through the lens of dominant philosophies, it is suggested to view them as "isms" considering that there are many different approaches within each of the three categories.

I chose to focus on the dominant modernist and postmodernist philosophies as they pertain to *Aloha*, storytelling, spirituality, and leadership.

The two dominant philosophical approaches related to Modernism (1650s to 1950s) include empiricism (knowing through the senses, which transitioned into scientific empiricism or modern science) and reason (or logic). Many times, reason and science were associated with each other.

Postmodernism included a questioning of previous approaches to knowing. Advocating epistemological pluralism (utilizing multiple ways of knowing) was preferred over relying on one approach to knowing. These pluralisms included premodern ways (i.e., revelation), modern ways (i.e., reason and science), and many other ways of knowing, including relational and spiritual intuition.

Leadership development in the upcoming decades will require a paradigm shift from the current self-centered way of being to a highly synergetic, united way with a heightened sense of connectedness. It has also been noted that this paradigm shift and spiritual growth spurt will lead to challenges related to value systems, relationships, and the ability to problem solve as humans evolve from a modernistic to a post-modernistic awareness. A heightened sense of spirituality will be a part of and a result of our evolution into the new paradigm.

Evolving from a Modern to a Postmodern Paradigm

The evolutionary road from a modern to a postmodern paradigm will be dramatically different than the previous evolutionary transition from the pre-modern to the modern paradigm. Leadership with an awareness of the transition from one paradigm to the next has been and will continue to be essential to the human evolutionary process.

Modern paradigm was dominated by theories generated by Newton, Kant, and Marx, while the pre-modern paradigm was based on fundamental beliefs catalyzed by Dante, Aquinas, and Augustine.

The modern paradigm was catalyzed by a series of revolutions, including geographic (Colonialism), intellectual (the Renaissance, modern science, and the Enlightenment period), economic (capitalism), political (bourgeois democracy), technological (the Industrial Revolution), in addition to artistic (modernism).

Postmodern theory suggests that a change in paradigm related to the view of reality originated from Einstein's work on relativism and quantum theory. Postmodern paradigm includes a negotiable reality where there is co-creation of perceptions of reality and layers of perceptions of constructs of reality called hyper-reality.

Rather than viewing one's world and values through the modern paradigm lens shaped by traditional world economics and religious systems, postmodern theory challenges each person to consciously lift the veils of personal bias and consciously create a humanitarian-centered reality where universal values are discussed and negotiated in terms of subjective rather than objective language.

It has also been suggested that the postmodern theory takes into account the fact that the observer affects the observed and that all of the cosmos is connected. With time, fear, and limitations, such as scarcity and isolation, will be replaced with a heightened awareness of abundance and connectivity as humans evolve into a postmodern paradigm.

The postmodern paradigm will give humans the opportunity to create a world of peace with a prosperous society that lives in balance with nature. Enlightenment and democracy guided by the vision of a just, egalitarian, participatory, ecological, healthy, and happy future are possible with the postmodern paradigm.

Leadership assisting in the transition from the modern to the postmodern paradigm embracing social responsibility will gravitate to a heightened awareness of spirituality via heightened awareness of connectivity with each other, the earth, and the universe.

Relationship Shifts and Social Responsibility

As the modern paradigm embraces negotiable relationships, how individuals see themselves as individuals and communities will be directly enlightened by their perceptions of the possibility, connectedness, and heightened awareness of spirituality.

Humans are consoled and strengthened by being together. Synergy, the creative energy of people working and living together, is the key to this shift of awareness. People do not need to know the exact outcomes of their actions, and they can live beyond their fears. All people really need is each other. The ability to feel synergy when in the co-creative mindset results from the awareness of connectivity and heightened spiritual awareness.

In the postmodern paradigm, humans are not dependent on the hope of results measured objectively. Heightened senses and intelligence, including spirituality and intuition, will open the gateway to the ability to experience and create beyond previously limiting perceptions of the world structured by measurable senses.

Communities operating in modern paradigms will notice over time that their work may appear worthless and even achieve no result due to the shift in perceptions of relationships with each other. Human interactions and relationships that originally catalyzed the creation of policies change over time and result in outdated policies that, in some cases, become destructive of the very relationships they were created to enhance or protect.

Heightened awareness of connectedness and humanitarianism are the keys to survival as a human species and one of the characteristics of a quiet leader. Humans gradually struggle less and less for an idea and more and more for specific people with the awareness that, in the end, it is the reality of personal relationships that saves everything. The ability to develop personal and negotiable relationships is the essence of social responsibility and the result of a heightened awareness of spirituality.

Spirituality

The perception of spirituality is affected by personal experiences and cultural influences. The common thread of spirituality is connectedness with other human beings, nature, and/or a possible Higher Power or Spiritual Guide expressed as variations of LOVE such as: Universe, Great Spirit, God, Creator, Shiva, Gaia, Jesus, Amaterasu, Buddha, Yu-Huang, Akal Murat, Allah, Shangdi, Tangaroa, Rod, Braham, Hera,

Zeus, Mother Mary, Abba, Pele, El Shaddai, Yahweh, Ha Shem, Holy Spirit… to name a few.

Spirituality is perceived and expressed in ways that are personal to each individual. The practices of *Aloha* (aka unconditional love) and forgiveness are common elements in the practice of spirituality expressed in many cultures and religious paths.

Aloha can be perceived as a universal language of spirituality, unifying the human experience striving for unity and love. Spirituality is sometimes described as the awareness of the force between the soul and personality. Spirituality is also described as the process of every human soul fulfilling with a Creator their sacred contract that was created prior to each human arriving here on earth.

Aloha unites and complements all spiritual paths, which embrace love, forgiveness, and harmony. It is in this awareness that we are able to recognize our common human nature and join our efforts in healing ourselves individually, as well as globally, along with healing our precious home, Earth.

In some circles, spirituality is the awareness of a human's personality aligning with their own soul, resulting in less turbulence in life. To some, humans co-create with each other, with or without their Creator, situations that align their soul with their purpose in life. As a whole, catalyzed by the challenges we all feel NOW (whether or not we believe in a Higher Power), our spiritual-human *ohana* (global family) is evolving.

From recent scientific evidence that points to a perceived human biological evolution involving a more developed corpus callosum (resulting in enhanced bridging of the left and right hemispheres of our brain, providing us with more developed abilities of perceiving and co-creating reality), it is believed that we, as a species in general, are becoming more capable of a higher awareness of **compassion** and **holistic thinking**.

This aligns with my hope that at this time in history, WE (the people of Earth) are physically, mentally, emotionally, as well as spiritually evolving and consciously coming together as a global *ohana* (family) to live and work together in harmony. I believe our conscious and unconscious practice of *Aloha* (love) is galvanizing this gloriously harmonious evolution.

YES! We (the evolving spiritual humans on this earthly journey together right now) are rising with *Aloha* (love) from our fragmented slumber states, co-creating a more peaceful, hopeful, joyful future for our children and future generations.

Summary

It is assumed that *Aloha* depends on a belief in a Higher Power; however, it is not exclusive to the belief of a Higher Power. It is possible to blend the concepts of *Aloha* being a protocol to the postmodern perception of a negotiable reality and *Aloha* being the language of universal spirituality. *Aloha* (love) can be practiced by individuals with or without a belief in a Higher Power.

Aloha is described in many ways with the common thread of universal love manifested in a desire for higher ethical behavior such as caring, cooperation, and unity catalyzed by self-reflection. As Sanskrit is the ancient language of emotions, *Aloha* can be perceived as a universal language of spirituality that illustrates universal spiritual values.

CHAPTER THREE

Aloha Stories

♥ ♥ ♥

"Aloha" is our unifying LOVE expressed in harmony with compassion, reverence, self-reflection, forgiveness, and patience.

~ Dr. Carole Aloha Hope Lockard

Throughout my observations and conversations with Pono Shim, my heart, mind, and soul opened to this universal process of sharing our authentic *Aloha* stories rooted in our daily practice of the *Aloha* values.

It fascinated me to observe (in myself and in other people) how the daily practice of *Aloha* evolves into our authentic *Aloha* stories, which connect us with each other in addition to helping us heal. By lifting our energy, conversations, relationships above discourse and debate, our *Aloha* stories transform us all to higher energetic/spiritual levels. Sharing our authentic *Aloha* stories with each other enables us to metaphorically sit on the same side of the table together, peacefully resolving our challenges.

As Pilahi Paki instructed Pono Shim to be a storyteller (telling stories in the old ways of connections — from heaven's perspective), Pono emphasized to me that our stories of *Aloha* come from one's own practice of the values of *Aloha*. Telling other people's *Aloha* stories does not resonate as strongly as telling one's own *Aloha* stories.

To clarify, our *Aloha* stories are neither to be preconceived for business or self-serving purposes nor forms of manipulation (intended to sway people's opinions to meet one's agenda). *Aloha* stories are truly a heart-to-heart sharing of wisdom through the soulful art of storytelling from people who practice *Aloha* daily. That is the essence of *Aloha* stories!

At a basic human level, writing about my *Aloha* stories via this book without physically meeting you (the reader) initially challenged me because I had not yet been blessed with the opportunity to get to know you or feel your heart's energy. Not having "talked story" with you (listening to your stories and sharing my stories with you) initially made me feel uncomfortable attempting to share my authentic and personal *Aloha* stories with you in this book. When I was guided in choosing to view things from an expansive and connected heaven's perspective, I realized it was not difficult at all.

From the authentic spirit of sharing my *Aloha* stories with you, I intend to be in the moment, energetically channeling my *Aloha* via storytelling while visualizing you as my younger, same-age, and older versions of myself. Believing that we are truly all connected (*Lō kahi*), I feel spiritually/energetically that we are one, experiencing our chosen cosmic and human life lessons within various realms of possibility with time in addition to space being relative. Ironically, this gives the concept of talking to myself a colossally different meaning. Considering the expansive and connective related theories of quantum physics with multi-dimensions of reality, it makes this process easier for me to share my *Aloha* stories with you, being right here, right now.

Since I was seven years old first learning about the *Aloha* values (originated from Pilahi Paki and initially shared with me by my hula teacher, Lorraine Brandt), I considered (and still consider) myself to be an Ambassador of Aloha, practicing daily the values of *Aloha* and sharing my authentic *Aloha* stories with others when guided to do so.

Accepting that I am not perfect at this integrative practice and make mistakes quite often, I am becoming more compassionate with myself on my journey. Fortunately, when I do fall in my practice of *Aloha*, I get back up and keep going. It is a process!

At this time, what I am guided to share with you is my *Aloha* story pertaining to the day I first heard Pono Shim speak at Argosy University (months prior to me asking Pono to be the subject of my case study for my research dissertation). This story also includes my first experience hearing Pono speak about the values of *Aloha* on the lawn of the Iolani Palace and subsequent experiences.

First Impressions

About thirteen years ago, while setting up a conference room for an Argosy University, Hawaii guest speaking event, I was very busy assisting in the last-minute preparations for the food, water, and chairs necessary for the gathering. This preparation process began immediately after I had ended my workday as the school's receptionist. It had been a long, full day at work for me, and I did not know who the guest speaker was going to be. I just knew there would be a guest speaker, and I arrived early to help set up the event room.

Sometime during this room preparation process, Pono entered the conference room and walked in my direction as I was setting up chairs in the front of the room. I initially thought Pono was a university staff member, student, or local business participant of the event.

After introducing myself, I welcomed Pono to the event, and offered him a glass of water and refreshments, which I had just started to set up a few minutes earlier. Handing a plastic cup of water to Pono, I invited him to sit close to the guest speaker's table (not knowing he WAS the guest speaker).

Pono kindly introduced himself and mentioned that he was the guest speaker for the event. Embarrassed by my ignorance, I apologized and invited him to sit at the center of the head table. He put his glass of water and folder on the table as he started to talk with people entering the conference room. I continued to set up the food, water, and chairs.

A few minutes passed, and I remember Pono, standing in front of the head table, speaking without a microphone, inviting guests to the meeting to sit close to the front of the room. While I was at the back of the room restocking the food and water tables, Pono introduced himself to the group. During the process of replenishing the refreshments, I looked up and was surprised to see that there were so many people in the room for the presentation. It was standing room only.

Suddenly, someone had caused a water spill at one of the water tables, and I rushed over to help clean it up, offering napkins to the people affected by the spill while using paper towels to soak up the water from the rug.

Everyone in the room was quiet as Pono continued to speak. I only understood some of what Pono was saying because I was busy with my hands and felt distracted. Continuing to soak up the water from the rug, I felt frustrated because I needed to hurry with this process so people around me would stop stepping on my hands.

When I thought I heard my first name spoken, I stopped what I was doing and looked up. Unable to identify the source of my spoken name, I went back to soaking up the water from the rug. Then I heard my name again and this time, I looked behind me at the front of the room where the crowd had parted, leaving me a direct view of Pono. While I was pointing to myself, Pono nodded and continued talking to the group.

Thinking Pono was requesting another cup of water, I stood up, placed the soaked paper towels in the nearby trash can, and grabbed a cup of water from the water table on my way to the front of the room. Pono shook his head when I offered him the cup of water. While pointing to an empty chair at the speaker's table, he said, "There is a space for you." Pono continued speaking to the people present in the room.

I quickly placed the water cup at the open spot on the speaker's table where I would sit and dashed over to the pastries station to grab my backpack, which I had stashed under the table concealed by its floor-length tablecloth.

Not processing what Pono was talking about while I was pulling out my notebook and pen from my backpack, I sat at the front table. My mind was racing with many thoughts as I settled into my chair. Not focused on what Pono was saying, I thought, *Was it okay for me to sit at the head table? University teachers were sitting there, and I was just a student!*

Taking a few sips of the water, followed by a couple of deep belly breaths, I began to calm down and process what Pono was saying related to his Aunty Pilahi Paki and his father, Alvin Shim. It was then that I began to understand, story after story, what Pono was sharing about his childhood, his family, and the people of Hawaii, all of whom he loved dearly.

Pono suddenly shifted gears, generally describing a few people in the conference room he had observed as he entered earlier that evening. He was curious about these people who appeared to be busy making themselves seen, telling people their titles and what type of work they did. The room became uncomfortably silent. I could feel people around me shift to shallow breathing.

Then, something energetically changed in the room and in me. I could hear my heartbeat in my ears, and for a few moments, all other sounds were blocked. Before I could process Pono's words, I closed my eyes and took a few deep breaths, which allowed me to slowly understand Pono's words. Without Pono mentioning any names, it sounded like Pono was describing me hectically (like a chicken without a head) preparing the conference room when he arrived. Some of the people in the room were laughing with his description. I felt embarrassed and frustrated, mainly because I did not feel comfortable receiving unwanted attention and possibly being the focus of a joke.

I was feeling anxious and not processing spoken words very well, so I wrote in my notebook the words that I was able to understand, doodling various geometric shapes (including elliptical drawings similar to the Spirograph game I played with as a child) to help me reduce my anxious feelings. When Pono mentioned that this person he had been observing (whom I thought might be me) was doing their best to help other people, I felt relieved, and my anxiety-provoked doodling subsided. My heart and breath began to return to a relaxed state. When I finally let out a big, quiet sigh (with a large exhale lowering my shoulders), I smiled, feeling grateful that without being singled out by name, my efforts in helping to set up the room and assisting guests were appreciated.

Pono then effortlessly tied his two previously mentioned observations together with clarification intertwined with his "watch me" and "see me" stories. Without any visual aids or a microphone, Pono captured the attention of everyone in the room, including me. Pono walked around the room and kept returning to the layers of meanings interwoven within the values of *Aloha*, originally taught to him by his great aunt, Pilahi Paki.

At that time, I did not recognize Pilahi Paki's name. I did, however, recognize the values of *Aloha* Pono was describing related to the *Aloha* values, which I had been taught originally by my childhood hula teacher, Lorraine Brandt.

Around this time, Pono asked the parents in the room to raise their hands. Many people raised their hands. Pono then shared a story of his daughter learning how to ride a bicycle without training wheels, describing how his daughter repeatedly said, "Watch me!" as she started to get the hang of it.

People in the audience, including myself, laughed. Then Pono asked for another show of hands, this time of the people who have had similar experiences with their children and/or parents. Almost every hand in the room went up.

Pono's next story described how he quietly entered his daughter's room when she was asleep to whisper in her ear how much he loved her and how grateful he felt for her being his daughter. The room became very quiet.

He then asked the parents in the room to raise their hands if they ever whispered gentle, loving words into their children's ears when their children were sleeping (or remember their parents whispering gently loving words into their ears and/or their siblings' ears when they were fast asleep).

With sounds of sniffling and napkins being crumpled after being used to wipe tears, most hands in the room were raised. Pono then suggested that the "Watch me!" words from their children may be coming from the children's need for attention, recognition, and/or direction, while the loving words whispered by parents into their children's ears as they slept reflected the parent's efforts in sharing their love for the child and spiritually/energetically saying, "I see you."

Pono clarified that the gentle, loving words parents whisper into their children's ears when they are sleeping may be coming from that place in the parents where they are clearly able to "see" with their hearts and not their eyes, the nature of their children and themselves, as what each of them truly are — LOVE!

You could have heard a pin drop. Then, there were sounds of people clearing their throats and sniffling. I started to tear up, recalling my similar personal experiences with my daughter, my parents, and my observations of my parents with my siblings. Through his storytelling, Pono touched and connected (Lō kahi) with all of us in that room that night.

Pono's timing was amazing! Now I understand that he was practicing the value of *Lō kahi* (connected, never broken) by gently opening people up to a connecting human experience of being a parent and a child, using his own authentic life stories related to "Watch me!" and "I see you," rooted in his daily practice of the *Aloha* values.

Time ran out, and Pono needed to leave for another engagement. He thanked everyone for participating in the experience. He ended the session with an open invitation for all present to a weekly noon *Aloha* values discussion he had recently started to facilitate on the lawn of Iolani Palace, located in the heart of Honolulu right next to Argosy University. I felt the energy of the people in the room being elevated.

Warm-heartedly, I observed participants of that night's guest speaking experience hugging each other and sincerely shaking hands.

Before Pono left the room, he stopped at the area where I was giving away leftover refreshments in the back of the room to guests who were leaving. Pono personally invited me to join the small weekly gathering on the lawn of Iolani Palace to discuss the *Aloha* values. He asked me if I was interested in participating in the group discussions. The next meeting was in two days. I felt honored and respectfully said yes.

On the day of my first meeting with the group, I only knew the meeting's time and general location. The Iolani Palace lawn was huge, and I trusted my guidance to lead me to the actual place of the gathering.

On my way through the Iolani Palace entrance gate, I noticed litter (paper napkins, plastic water bottles, and a few plastic food containers) on the ground where I was walking. I picked up the trash and threw it away in a nearby trash can. Squirting a bit of hand sanitizer (that was clipped to one of the straps on my backpack) onto my hands, I cleaned them while walking forward.

A few people waved their hands to me from a small group seated on lawn chairs under a tree, so I continued walking in their direction. I did not have a chair, just a small towel I had placed in my backpack to put the fruit containers on. Thinking it was a potluck lunch meeting, I brought to share cut-up pieces of pineapple, papaya, starfruit, guava, and a bunch of small apple bananas, which came from my yard and a family member's yard.

I walked up to the group and noticed that the beach chairs were arranged in a half circle. I asked Pono if he was expecting more people. He said yes and remarked that he intended to create a circle with all the participants after everyone arrived.

Yes, I naturally thought it was a potluck gathering, with the meeting starting at noon. As it turned out, I quickly learned that it was not a potluck as more people arrived without food to share. I was not worried. There was plenty of fruit for everyone to enjoy.

Feeling comfortable and useful, I introduced myself and "talked story" to those present in the group while passing out paper products, toothpicks, and pieces of fruit.

The air smelled sweet with the mixed fragrance of the fruit we were eating and the nearby flowers. Pono finished eating his fruit, drank some water, and began with storytelling involving his parents and family. I remember feeling inspired by Pono's apparent vulnerability in sharing his personal, heartfelt stories related to his everyday life, work, and family.

Pono then reviewed highlights of the values of *Aloha* as they were taught to him by his great aunt Pilahi Paki, briefly integrating his evolving perspective, as well as a few short stories illustrating his daily practice of the *Aloha* values. When he was done sharing, he drank some water and graciously invited people in the group to share what we were guided to share.

There was a long, silent pause, with most people looking down at the ground. I could hear my heartbeat increasing in volume and speed in my chest and my ears. I noticed I was sitting in the shade of the tree with a gentle cool breeze moving the branches and starting to feel warm. Energetically/intuitively, I sensed it was time for me to share.

The two people next to me offered me napkins as tears started to roll down my cheeks when the words began to flow from my mouth. I felt safe and accepted by Pono and the whole group to open up and trust the flow of my words, which I was intuitively being guided to share at that time.

The words that flowed out of my mouth intermingled with tears and a runny nose. Because I felt a mixture of strong emotions surfacing while sharing my story, I did not have much clarity of thought. Words and emotions seemed to blend in my awareness, yet my heart and soul knew that I could trust my guidance and this group in continuing to share until I was guided to stop.

When my multiple-layered emotions bubbling up inside of me started to feel overwhelming, I paused, closed my eyes, and took a few deep belly breaths. I also firmly massaged with my thumb and pointer finger of my right hand the muscle of my left hand's palm between my thumb and pointer finger). While my emotions quieted down, I continued to share my evolving story.

What initially emerged out of me were brief gratitude stories of my family, centering around my love for my mother (who was my relatively new heavenly angel). I dearly missed Mom's presence with me on earth! I could feel her spiritual presence in all I did, including sharing this story during the gathering (as I do now, writing this story).

My mother was a quiet leader of the women in my family. In addition, Mom's community leadership roles, prior to being the mother of six children, included being a lead flight attendant for Hawaiian Airlines, while being the part-time Office Administrator for Hawaiian Telephone Company's CEO.

While the six of us kids were growing up, Mom's leadership roles included being one of the first Girl Scout Leaders in Hawaii, serving as our parish's sodality leader for many years, working full time as the Religious Education Director of St. John Vianney School for over a decade, followed by being the Alumni Director of Maryknoll High School (long before she was formally paid for her service in that role). Mom's employment at our schools helped subsidize our tuition at each school.

My mother was known for being a revered friend and mentor. My siblings and I knew her as Mom, who was always there for us and forever encouraging us to be of service while pursuing our dreams. Her efficient productivity, leadership, resourcefulness, generosity of heart, and gentle kindness made her the "go-to" person in her circles to catalyze change and get things done while being there for others. Yes, Mom enjoyed a full and rewarding life here on earth filled with many joyful blessings! She passed away after a long struggle with breast cancer and became my family's and my guardian angel at her tender earthly age of 58 (the same age I am now, in this moment, sharing this story with you, my Reader).

My main message to the group was of gratitude and reverence for my mom. When Pono talked about the *Aloha* values, my mother and how she lived her life came to my mind. Mom was my first (and still is my most impactful) Ambassador of Aloha mentor, who, for me, truly embodied and still embodies **all** of the values of *Aloha*.

The short story that followed from deep inside of me described my love for Granny Cabral (Adeline Vivian Marks Cabral), my maternal grandmother (another one of my current heavenly angels and spiritual Aloha Ambassador mentors). When my mother returned to work, my grandmother helped care for us six kids, especially the children who were sick and needed to stay home from school. In addition, my daughter and I lived with Granny for about 7 years during her memory decline after my mother passed away.

Suddenly, what emerged were my feelings of frustration regarding my family members' denial related to my grandmother's increasing memory loss challenges, as well as their supportive efforts to help care for her during the tough years. Everyone was doing the best they could with the time and resources they had available to them.

You see, Granny hid her memory loss struggles. Living with my grandmother for many years, my daughter and I saw first-hand the signs of her memory slowly slipping away, such as noticing Granny periodically leaving her checkbook in the refrigerator or placing canned beans in her bathroom cabinet next to the bleach container and the toilet paper. When I brought up our observations and experiences to my family, our experiences were minimalized.

At first, my daughter and I observed small slips in Granny's memory, such as forgetting the names of the people she knew for decades and sometimes calling my daughter and me by other people's names. Towards the end of our seven years of living with Granny, her memory loss challenges were painfully pronounced. There was a series of health and safety-related events (with police involvement and emergency visits to Castle Hospital), which led to my grandmother finally being diagnosed with dementia and Alzheimer's disease.

My grandmother's diagnosis finally broke through my family's denial of her mental illness. The doctor said Granny needed 24/7 care, which led to my grandmother being moved into a care home in Kailua that was run by earthly angels (a local nurse and her kind-hearted family). Throughout it all, I witnessed my family members' constant efforts to do their best to care for Granny in their own way and in their own time. It was a true family effort!

Being the eldest granddaughter, I felt obligated to continue taking care of my grandmother, even though I knew I did not have the time or the resources to do so full-time. It broke my heart watching my grandmother's memory deteriorate over the years, followed by Granny needing to be moved out of her home for her health and safety.

My emotions were raw at this point of telling my story, and I was guided to stop. It was then that the group came alive with individuals, one by one, sharing their *Aloha* stories related to their *kapuna* (elderly) parents, grandparents, family members, and loved ones who struggled with dementia, Alzheimer's disease, and/or other forms of mental illness. They also shared their love for their family members who did their best in providing quality care (honoring the dignity of their beloved *kapuna* and the caretaker family members) each in their own unique ways and timing.

While people in the group shared what was in their hearts, a few members (including me) started making connections between the values of *Aloha* and the stories emerging from each of us. It was exciting to see the values of *Aloha* evolve out of our impromptu authentic personal stories. The lights were turning on in each of us! After participating in this connective "talk-story" process, sharing common emotionally charged human experiences, we felt a common bond with each other. We began to weave together the values of *Aloha* that were emerging from our individual and collective stories. It was beautiful!

The stories shared by the members in the circle were just as fascinating as Pono's stories. I thoroughly enjoyed being a part of this group experience... until Pono did it again!

It was time to end the meeting. I needed to return to work as the receptionist at my university across the street from the gathering, as did others in the group who needed to return to their work locations in downtown Honolulu. I started collecting the trash from the group members, using an additional plastic bag I had in my backpack. At the same time, Pono reminded everyone about upcoming events and the next meeting.

Then, Pono brought the group's attention to his description of a person he had observed picking up trash on the lawn before the meeting. I wondered if Pono was referring to me, and I felt self-conscious, even though he neither mentioned my name nor looked at me. Folding the small towel and putting my pen and notebook in my backpack, I kept my gaze down.

Thank God/LOVE/Universe Pono quickly shifted the topic of his closing remarks to the importance of the *Aloha* values, connecting people with each other and all that exists, including the *aina* — (that which feeds... the land and the sea).

Pono briefly reminded us of our homework, which was to practice the *Aloha* values daily. While the group was dispersing and after I finished a conversation with a group member, Pono folded up his beach chair, waited for me to look up from putting my things in my backpack, and said, "I see you." Feeling initially surprised by his comment and then gratitude, I respectfully responded with *Mahalo*.

That was the beginning of about five Iolani Palace *Aloha* values group discussions. The discussions stopped when Pono's work schedule did not allow for more lunchtime meetings. A couple of months later, Pono agreed to be the subject of my dissertation's case study, which was required to complete my doctorate degree.

I greatly respected Pono and felt honored that he was willing to mentor me while assisting me with my dissertation process.

Aloha Values Evolving Into *Aloha* Stories

Pono mentioned to me during our many dissertation-related observations and events that the values of *Aloha* cannot (and should not) be practiced or taught isolating each value from the other (except in an introductory manner) because the values themselves are connected.

When Pono initially shared the values of *Aloha* with me for my formal research dissertation process, he gave me an introduction to the values, reviewing what Pilahi Paki had taught him, layered his perspectives of the deeper meanings of the values individually and then blended with the other *Aloha* values.

Pono clarified that similar to other words in the Hawaiian language, the words Pilahi Paki chose to describe the *Aloha* values had layers of meanings that intertwined with each other. Pono said that it is our *kuleana* (responsibility) to discover for ourselves the deeper meanings of the values rooted in our individual and our shared human experiences, uncovered in our daily practice of *Aloha*.

It took a while for me to understand that our unique perceptions of the *Aloha* values are highly individual and humanly universal. It took me even longer to experience how our *Aloha* stories evolve from our daily practice of *Aloha*... not the other way around.

At first, I felt my head swirling when I heard Pono talk about the interweaving of *Aloha* values by sharing our authentic *Aloha* stories with others. My intention for my dissertation (focused on *Aloha*, storytelling, and leadership) was linear/logical by the nature of a doctorate-level case study and literature review research process, mandated by my dissertation research requirements.

Being a circular thinker and communicator, describing matters of the heart and soul, how could I fully understand (and then explain to others in a straightforward linear way) the processes involved in learning the *Aloha* values and creating *Aloha* stories? I felt overwhelmed by this daunting question! How could something be so individual and universal at the same time? During the beginning of my dissertation research process, the duality and complexity involved with this process were, at times, overwhelming.

I also felt my role as a researcher was to create a clear research-based process for myself and others to understand and practice the *Aloha* values and *Aloha* stories based on my observations and interviews of/with Pono. As it turns out, in my fumbling efforts of practicing the *Aloha* values and sharing my *Aloha* stories with others, I began to understand what Pono was talking about with my heart and soul.

You see, I had it all backwards from the start! It is in the daily practice of the *Aloha* values that our *Aloha* stories emerge, not trying to understand the *Aloha* values with our minds in order to connect them to our life stories. It is also the sharing of our *Aloha* stories with each other (emerging from our unique, authentic practices of the *Aloha* values) that we begin to feel connected, recognizing the brilliance of love in ourselves and others. In accepting this paradox and simplicity (gift-wrapped in the messiness of life), we graciously lean into 'being' *Aloha* with our heart and soul, rather than trying to understand *Aloha* with our mind.

Starting to finally see the light when I began to let go of trying to understand it all with my brain, I leaned into feeling with my heart/soul this interconnected process. When I make this journey of assimilating this wisdom from my head to my heart/soul… It is simple! Our daily practice of the *Aloha* values unconsciously and innately shapes our *Aloha* stories, while sharing our *Aloha* stories helps us clarify our *Aloha* values, which in turn helps us feel harmoniously connected with each other.

Now, I am guided to share my experiences related to the setting up process of my Aloha Stories LLC business (including writing this book), which will illustrate my unique perspectives and practice of the *Aloha* values intertwined with my sharing of my *Aloha* stories.

After over a decade of sharing complementary (free of charge) *Aloha* values introduction sessions and my *Aloha* Stories' perspectives with local as well as global families, organizations, and businesses, this past February, I formally started my Aloha Stories LLC business in Hawaii, including beginning my journey of publishing this (my first) book based on my research dissertation.

Thinking I could quickly learn what I needed to know about setting up and running an LLC business and self-publishing my book, I did my best to obtain the information I needed to resolve my multiplying business challenges. During the worldwide COVID pandemic isolation period, I dove deep into online classes and support discussion groups to obtain the information, skill sets, and support needed to grow my business and publish my book, with the intention of gifting myself time to relax after my business was well established.

To say the least, my body, mind, and soul rebelled with this inhumane approach of pushing myself to start and build my education and Aloha Stories LLC consulting business, along with publishing my book. I had slipped in my daily practice of the *Aloha* values, especially the value of *Aka hai*. My whole being was out of balance.

AKA HAI

Pilahi Paki defined ***Aka hai*** as "**kindness** to be expressed with **tenderness.**" With Pono's guidance, the deeper meaning for me evolved into treating each person (including myself) as if they (I) were a baby, accepting the good, the bad, and the messy of all aspects of others (along with myself) with kindness, gentleness, and tenderness.

It has been about six months since I started this book's authoring process with the guidance of my trusted publisher. Initially, I intended to write a reader-friendly version of my research dissertation, honoring my mentor, Pono Shim. Over time, this book evolved to integrating my tribute to Pono (based on my research dissertation experiences) with what Pono had encouraged me to do (in my own voice and creative ways to share with others my *Aloha* stories that evolve out of my daily practice of *Aloha*). With this process of writing a book while setting up an LLC business being a new experience for me, I felt naive and vulnerable, like a child learning how to walk for the first time.

During the past few months of writing this book, I experienced many emotional peaks (including joy and excitement) and deep emotional valleys (including feelings of self-doubt and overwhelm). This emotional rollercoaster experience was partly due to my self-inflicted bouts of sleep deprivation, resulting from allowing myself to write when I felt guided to write, having no sense of time nor a healthy sleep routine).

I periodically found myself typing my thoughts and feelings into my laptop until the morning birds started to make themselves known outside of my window. It only took a couple of days of this free-wheeling, sleep-deprived writing process for me to go "splat" (borrowing Dr. Sue Morter's technical term describing my physical, mental, emotional, energetic, and spiritual crash experience).

Being blessed with an amazing Higher Power along with heavenly/earthly angels (including my Hawaii and global *ohana*) who collectively assisted me as I picked myself up from "splat," dusted myself off, regained balance, and kept moving forward by taking one step at a time. Inspired by LOVE, as well as my heavenly/earthly angels' practice of *Aka hai* with me during this transformational process I've been in, I choose to continue daily being *Aka hai* with myself, which manifests in me being *Aka hai* with others. The *Aka hai* circle of love lives long and prospers.

Feeling more self-compassion within myself and being reflected in my more harmonious relationships with others, I continue my daily *Aka hai* practices including:

- syncing my sleep routine with the birds
- sharing heart-to-heart hugs and belly laughs with others
- celebrating life during potluck meals full of "talk-story"
- dancing and singing like a two-year-old child
- playing in the ocean like a twirling dolphin
- locally/globally exploring nature with loved ones

My return to these and other daily self-nurturing *Aka hai* practices resulted in me treating myself (and subsequently others) with more kindness, complemented by tenderness, manifesting in me feeling more alive, creative, and grateful for my many blessings. As a bonus, my improved sleep quality was restored with more guided, joyful, insightful, and inspirational color dreams.

In essence, I was replenishing my metaphoric energetic cup to overflow by practicing *Aka hai*, enabling me to feel balanced and full, which gifted me the opportunity to give to others from abundance rather than from scarcity.

When I am not grounded in my practice of *Aloha* (specifically *Aka hai*... being kind and tender with myself), I become more sensitive to emotional triggers and feel more susceptible to my fears. In addition, I also see myself repeating old fear-based patterns, such as holding on tightly to the outcomes of my efforts, resulting in micromanaging myself and others.

Often, this unbalanced negative process manifests in me not caring for myself with a martyr mentality (sacrificing my health and well-being with my unbalanced efforts of serving others and/or the greater good) devastatingly impacting my ability to dream and realize life aspirations. In a nutshell, when I am not practicing *Aka hai*, everything (internally and externally) unravels quickly and becomes one big mess. When I am practicing Aka hai daily, internal and external harmony flows. I begin to feel balanced in all areas of my life.

STORY TIME . . .

My Grandpa DeMello (my father's father) gifted me a love of the ocean. One of my earliest memories with Grandpa was walking on Lanikai Beach behind Great Grandpa Rosa's beach home (one of the first homes built in Lanikai). I was about three years old. Grandpa did not talk much while he walked with me. He just held my hand while I walked in and through the gentle waves lapping my feet as we slowly strolled along the shoreline on the soft, fine white sand. Grandpa DeMello was a very tall (6 foot plus) athletic man with gentle eyes and a brilliant smile who loved his family and the ocean.

As we walked together from time to time, he would crouch down next to me and in his deep, gentle voice, ask me questions about what I saw, felt, smelled, heard, (and when safe) tasted related to the ocean and the creatures that lived in it, including the seaweed, shells, rocks, fish, crabs, Portuguese man o' war, jellyfish and green sea turtles. Back then, it was okay to touch the *honus* (turtles). I remember my Grandpa chuckling when I talked with the ocean and my new ocean friends, mimicking his way of talking with me.

Sometimes, he would sit with me on the sand as I rolled and played in the gentle waves, laughing when the waves splashed against my face and cringed when the water went in my mouth and nose. He taught me how to blow bubbles in the water and exhale the water out of my nose.

As I got a little older, Grandpa taught me how the ocean breathes like we breathe, moving water instead of air, in and out, in and out. He would place his forehead on my forehead and breathe slowly so I could feel and hear his breath syncing with mine. I thought that was fun and giggled. Grandpa's breath smelled like peppermint gum, which smelled good to me.

It thrilled me when Grandpa would swing me around with my feet kissing the waves in the water and when he put me on his shoulders while he moved in the water. As I became more comfortable in the ocean, Grandpa taught me how to swim, which involved going under the waves and floating on my back. At a very young age, I swam like a fish and absolutely loved being in the ocean, especially with Grandpa.

Grandpa put me in the family rowboat a few times and rowed me around the Mokulua Islands, telling me stories about the ocean creatures we saw moving through the water around and under us and on the reef. I was captivated by Grandpa's stories related to these beautiful sea creatures.

As I grew older, life got busy, and I spent less time alone with Grandpa. My siblings and I enjoyed family time and special adventures with Grandpa, especially when he came to our sports and school events. We also have fond memories of Grandpa driving us in his red and black 1942 Ford Model T Roadster (which he built from the ground up) around Kailua, as well as in island parades. It was a treat when Grandpa and I shared time together, and I cherish every moment.

Once, when I was around twelve, Grandpa took me to the left Mokulua Island, where we saw a green sea turtle sunbathing on the sand. No one was there, just the two of us on the island. As we pushed the boat onto shore, Grandpa explained to me how special the *honu* (turtle) was and how we needed to take extra care of all our ocean friends, especially the *honu*, the wisdom keepers of the sea.

As we approached this medium-sized wise soul, Grandpa reminded me that we needed to give it space to get used to us being there. So, we sat on the sand a few feet away, drinking water and enjoying the sun's warmth while watching the *honu* breathe. I remember Grandpa saying that we needed to treat all creatures and each other like babies because we all need each other like a baby needs its parents to protect and take care of it.

Like a *honu*, Grandpa said our hard shells help protect us from getting hurt but sometimes prevent us from getting close to others. He continued explaining that our underbelly softshells allow us to get close to each other and sometimes make us very vulnerable to getting hurt. When we help each other with tender love to soften our hard shells and with uplifting love to strengthen/toughen our softshell, we help each other find that balance of being kindhearted and giving while being discerning and aware of dangers.

From a distance, I saw the *honu* watching us and asked Grandpa if we could get closer. He said no because it was resting. Grandpa told a story of how the *honu*, especially around the Mokulua Islands, swam great distances around the islands and survived many challenges like being eaten by sharks, trapped in fishermen's nets, and caught by people. We needed to be kind and loving to these gentle creatures as we protect and nurture them because they are very wise and very vulnerable. He explained that the hard shells the *hono* have protect them to a certain point. Just like all other creatures, including us, they have weak areas where they need their other *honus*, other creatures, and us to help them.

I loved Grandpa's *honu* "car wash" story. During his many dives for *opihi* (shelled sea creature) and *tako* (octopus), Grandpa witnessed a certain coral reef area where the turtles mingle like workers at a car wash. The turtles would swim above this large coral reef with many sea anemones, and small fish would swarm around the honu, cleaning its shell and other parts of the turtle. I laugh every time I remember Grandpa's *honu* car wash story, visualizing the fish cleaning the *honus* with the 1976 "Working at the Car Wash" song by Rose Royce playing in my head.

When I reflect on my experiences with Grandpa and the stories he shared with me, I feel a deep appreciation for him, especially the lessons I now relate to Aka hai, resounding our daily practice of being kind, gentle, and tender with ourselves, each other and all that exists.

LŌ KAHI

When practicing the *Aloha* value of *Lō kahi* (as Pilahi Paki suggested, meaning "unity to be expressed with harmony" while viewing things from heaven's perspective, with Pono's added layer of meaning that we and all that exists are "connected…never broken"), I begin to clearly see the interwoven values of *Aloha* collectively in myself, everyone, my daily experiences, and …basically everything. Choosing to view myself, others, and life through heaven's perspective (with all sides evolving to one unifying side "love," not just two opposing sides considered) simplifies the whole process for me.

The highest level of understanding the multilayered meanings of *Lō kahi* was shared to me by Pono, through a metaphor including a Hawaiian flower lei with a string (symbolizing unconditional continuously flowing Love) connecting all the flowers (symbolizing all of us and everything that exists) in one beautiful circularly connected strand of flowers (lei of people and all that is).

In the ancient Hawaiian culture, leis were (and are sometimes still) constructed by weaving flowers together within tightly woven string-like parts of plants. This additional level of cultural lei creation adds to the metaphor by suggesting we are woven and sometimes strung together into one spiritual/energetic human LOVE *ohana* (family) lei.

Pono added that the deeper meaning of *Lō kahi* of being connected never broken refers to the concept that with the universal connector of *Aloha* (love), we were, have been, and forever will be connected… never broken. Many spiritual belief systems and quantum physics all resound this universal truth.

Expanding the meaning of this flower lei metaphor, in the Hawaiian culture, a lei is the symbol of an extended hug. When receiving or giving a lei made with love (including real/artificial/paper flowers, shells, seeds, ribbons, yarn, string, etc.), the lei you are receiving or gifting is a symbolic extension of one's energetic/spiritual *Aloha* (love), extended by one's physical hug. A lei is a beautiful multilayered physical, spiritual, energetic symbol and cultural practice related to *Lō kahi*.

Throughout the years, I have been blessed to have participated in many life celebrations (birthdays, anniversaries, graduations, etc.). During these celebrations (as is customary in the Hawaiian culture), I have received/given many Hawaiian leis from/to family and friends. I believe the *Aloha* (love) transferred to, from, and through us in these leis extends to all of us (and all that exists) throughout all of eternity, which is wholeheartedly in alignment with our unifying celebration of *Lō kahi*.

Many times during my writing of this book and my 2012 research dissertation, I felt the presence and guidance of God/LOVE/Universe and the multitudes of my heavenly angels who have gifted me with their *Aloha*. I know I am never alone. I have a very strong belief (a knowingness) that I am spiritually/energetically connected (never broken) with all that exists, especially my loved ones' past, present, and future. Feeling guided each step of the way, I truly appreciate the *Aloha* value of *Lō kahi*, which resonates strongly in and through me always, which I strongly feel NOW.

In my thoughts, intentions, actions, and verbal/written words that come out of me (for example, in the form of written words and stories in this book) when I am daily practicing *Aloha,* I feel a continuous connecting flow of higher vibration *Aloha* (love) energy. When I am in the flow of daily practicing *Aloha*, I am tuned into my soul's purpose, which is aligned with my personality in these times of practice.

This state of awareness and practice is reflected in my feeling that I am energetically vibrating at a higher frequency (LOVE) when I am in the flow practicing the values of *Aloha* daily. In this way of being, I feel connected in my spiritually human experiences (*Lō kahi*) with myself and all that exists here on earth and in heaven (all loving realms of our cosmos).

STORY TIME . . .

In every sense of the word, my Dad was an amazing practitioner of *Lō kahi*! My first memories of being with my father involved me feeling protected, celebrated, and included. From helping me learn how to discern and protect myself when I felt bullied to showing me how to share my stories in ways where I could pick up energy from others and interweave that information into my stories to connect with people. Dad was all about connecting!

When I was young, my father would bring coffee cans of screws, nuts, bolts, and washers, all mixed up and oily from the planes and crew members involved with his work as the Chief of Aircraft at Hawaii Air National Guard. As kids, my siblings and I called my Dad the "plane doctor." Dad explained that these coffee cans filled with "loose screws" (as he jokingly called them) were leftover tools from the "surgeries" (procedures) he and his crew performed when healing (fixing/maintaining) jets and planes in their care.

Dad was always looking for a volunteer to help him with projects in the yard and the garage. At around five years of age, one of the projects I volunteered for was sorting and organizing the "loose screws" in the coffee cans using the empty glass jars from baby food and preserved food items my mother had cleaned and stacked in boxes for Dad to use with this project. It was my job to sit on the ground in the garage and sort all that was in these large coffee cans into the glass jars of various sizes.

The first time I worked on this project, I cried. It was overwhelming, and I broke a few glass jars trying to get my work area organized. Dad came over from working under the hood of our family station wagon, cleaned up the broken glass, and gave me a hug. He told me to sit still and then brought a flat bedsheet from the house for me to sit on and use as my work area. After he spread out the sheet in the area of the garage that was out of his way, he helped me organize a few jars (strategically placed on the sheet) about arm's length from me, with a sample of each "loose screw" placed in front of each jar designated for collection.

As I was spreading out the bedsheet, looking at a turquoise ladybug that had landed on my arm, Dad went back into the house and brought out Mom's egg timer and a plastic cup of water. I drank the water while the ladybug flew away.

Before setting the timer, he told me this was a game. I felt excited! I loved games! Dad explained that if I could put as many of the similar "loose screws" into the designated jars by the time the timer rang (without taking a break or crying), he would take "the gang," including me, to Kailua Beach to play in the ocean with a big floaty plane tire inner tube. At that time, "the gang" (my core family) included 3 sisters, 1 brother, and my Mom. I was on a mission to win this game, not only for myself but also for "the gang." It was up to me!

Now remember, at five years of age, I did not know how to tell time, and Dad did not involve any numbers in his directions; he just wanted me to sort the "loose screws" into the designated glass jars by the time the timer rang (without taking a break or crying). I had no idea of the amount of time he set the timer for. Dad turned the radio on, and I began to work, bopping my head in time with the music. The game started when he said, "Go!" Before I knew it, the timer rang. Dad came over to where I was seated, lifted me up and twirled me in the air celebrating how good of a job I had done sorting the "loose screws."

Mom and my siblings flew out of the house and into our garage because of the commotion. Dad showed everyone what I had done and made me feel FANTASTIC! The gang piled into the station wagon with the big inner tube in the back section of the car, along with towels, our Igloo water jug, paper cups, sand toys, buckets, a sand net, snacks, Dad's first-aid kit, and Mom's baby bag.

While we were on our way to Kailua Beach, Dad turned up the radio as the theme song from Gilligan's Island (a popular television sitcom) was playing, and we all sang along. Dad magically turned a frustrating task for me into a fun game that ended up with a celebration involving our whole family. It was awesome!

Throughout elementary school, I kept volunteering for that "loose screws" project my father had waiting for me in a bucket on the floor of the garage closet. In time, I had emptied so many coffee cans (which were recycled in Dad's plant nursery as planters) and organized so many "loose screws" into hundreds of glass jars of various sizes that Dad built wooden shelves all along the edges of the garage within his arm's length while he stood on the ground, displaying all of MY "loose screw" jars that he chose to hold on to for safekeeping. The majority of the 'loose screw' jars were returned to work for his crew to recycle into their inventory.

Taking a time warp leap forward many years to the first day of my internship at Chaminade University's Montessori Preschool classroom, as a masters education student, I laughed and cried tears of gratitude when I saw all the different ways individual and group completed projects were celebrated, in addition to how items were sorted and organized in the classrooms, including "loose screws" in small plastic jars (similar to my Dad's "loose screws" baby jar sorting game).

Looking back, I can now see that while I was helping my dad with his "loose screws" game, he was helping me learn sorting and organizational life skills. Dad was also celebrating ME. In addition to my victory in the game, he included our whole family in the celebration. As I am writing this story/memory, tears of gratitude stream down my cheeks. Dad always said he was a man ahead of his time.

These are just a few memories I have when I was young, demonstrating my Dad's practice of *Lō kahi*. As I grew up and watched him interact with people, telling stories and evoking stories out of people, I was in awe at how effortlessly he connected with people. He first listened, observed, and then shared stories, which many times inspired the people he was with to share their stories.

The men my Dad mentored during the 35-plus years of service in the Hawaii Air National Guard (especially pilots and crew members) expressed to Dad and us (his family) how grateful they were for his guidance, protection, and inclusion in his *ohana* (family). Dad was constantly bringing men home from work (local men and men with no family on the island) to share family meals and holidays with us. My siblings and I enjoyed getting to know them and hearing about Dad's and their stories of traveling all around the world, helping people involved in devastating wars and natural disasters. Dad and these men became our superheroes!

Dad used to say, "What is important is not what you say or what you do, but rather the way you speak and act." Many times, he would reiterate that people remember how they feel being around you, not so much what you say and do. If they do not feel welcome and included via your energy, words, and actions, trust will not grow. Dad believed that we are ALL children of a loving God (universal higher power), and he taught us (his children) how to be *Lō kahi* (inclusive with discernment).

In reflection, I now see that my Dad's charismatic and down-to-earth personality, enhanced by his natural leadership gifts assisted him in being an outstanding leader in our core/extended family, work *ohana*, and community. I feel grateful that my Dad taught me, by example, how to be *Lō kahi* (always with discernment), including people (especially those less fortunate) honoring their dignity and listening with one's heart to people's stories.

OLU`OLU

In Pono's sharing of the deeper values of *Olu`olu* with me, I saw how heavily connected this value was (is) to the introspective (self-reflective) aspects of *Lō kahi* and *Ha`a ha`a*. Pilahi Paki described *Olu`olu* as meaning "agreeable to be expressed with pleasantness." Pono explained that the deeper meaning of *Olu`olu* was similar to a medical surgeon's practice of wearing gloves prior to and during surgery.

In the surgeon's efforts of *doing no harm* while helping the patient, the surgeon wears gloves to prevent bacteria on their hands from contaminating the field of surgery, as well as potentially harmful biological substances from the patient contaminating the surgeon. If the protective gloves are not worn, there could be potentially lethal harm done to the patient and the surgeon.

Pono further explained that these surgical gloves symbolically remind us to keep our egos, self-serving intentions, and agendas in check before and during our efforts to help others, whether it be a symbolic cleansing of a topical infection (internal strife or disagreement within oneself or someone), or a deeply rooted systemic carcinogenic condition (deterioration of an aspect of oneself or a family/organization). The gloves also symbolically remind us to be mindful of protecting ourselves from potential harm while helping others. The *do no harm* concept tied in with this metaphor applies to people we help and ourselves.

In our initial conversation regarding *Olu`olu,* the importance of trust, confidentiality, and preserving dignity arose. Pono explained that woven within the deeper meanings of *Olu`olu* were layers of these three disciplines. *Doing no harm* while assisting ourselves and others on our healing journeys is easier to do when these principles are honored.

Pono clarified that trust with oneself and others is built on one thought, one word, and one action at a time. Regarding trust, Pono referred to inner trust with oneself and outer trust with others. He said trust is a lifelong process that ebbs and wanes. The most important part of trust is being willing to build and repair trust, which requires an open heart, openness to inner and external guidance, forgiveness, and balance with discernment (needed to create and maintain healthy boundaries while repairing broken trust).

Pono quickly added that when trust (especially confidentiality is broken) with oneself and/or others, practicing forgiveness in whatever spiritual/energetic form one is familiar with and comfortable practicing is helpful. Pono clarified that it is helpful for this forgiveness process to include self-introspection, asking for forgiveness, and making amends (which are forgiveness aspects in many spiritual practices, including the *Ho`oponopono* process mentioned in the *Ha`a ha`a* section).

Focusing on confidentiality, Pono explained that *doing no harm* involved in the practice of *Olu`olu* includes honoring the dignity of our own stories and other peoples' stories. Pono emphasized this point by stating that sharing other people's stories (or sharing our own stories in a way that does not preserve the dignity of other people involved) is not *pono* (not right).

When sharing our own stories, Pono said that remembering Aunty Pilahi's suggestion of telling stories from heaven's perspective is crucial to preserving people's dignity, and this only comes from the daily practice of the *Aloha* values.

What came to mind for me while hearing Pono's words of wisdom was the golden rule, "Do unto others as you would want others to do unto you." Storytelling about other people without the practice of *Olu`olu* (helping others while not preserving people's dignity) many times leads to harmful gossip and damaged relationships. In the practice of *Olu`olu*, it is best to let other people share their own *Aloha* stories and sparingly share parts of other people's stories as they relate to your story in ways that "prosper" (lift and celebrate) them while honoring their dignity.

Pono continued explaining how important it is to preserve our own and other people's dignity by not letting our egos get in our way (meaning we need to follow our inner/external guidance, heart, and soul in balance with our mind) when we find ourselves in opportunities of being conscious of heaven's perspective (with all sides included) and choosing whether to intercede in our own and other people's growth/healing processes, especially when a crisis is occurring.

Pono reminded me of the Japanese kanji characters "danger" and "opportunity," which are combined in the kanji symbol that translates to mean "crisis." He said, especially when a crisis involves loved ones, it takes the strength of our cumulative daily practice of this *Aloha* value to be mindful of the possibility of our ego, motives, and judgments possibly "contaminating the field of surgery."

We need to symbolically put our *Olu`olu* surgical gloves on and proceed with caution, responding with love rather than reacting from fear (soulful guidance rather than mind-driven ego), aware that the crisis at hand can be dangerous and is also an opportunity to heal, learn and grow individually in addition to collectively. All involved in the crisis have opportunities to be a part of each other's healing processes at multiple levels.

When we practice daily the values of *Aloha*, we develop the energetic/spiritual muscle of taking that *pause* for introspection and openness to guidance, which is necessary to have clarity of our inner and external guidance that will assist us in making "clean" choices (meaning *doing no harm* from heaven's perspective) that sometimes includes **not** offering unsolicited advice, assistance and/or sharing our perceptions.

Pono confirmed that sometimes this *Olu`olu* practice involves a conscious choice to not intercede in another person's healing process, to honor their noble choices in their life journey, and to empower them to make their own mistakes necessary for their healing and growth.

With laser focus, Pono shared his perception of his Aunty Pilahi's words, "It is in that pause, 'the width of a blade of pili grass' where we are guided to respond from *Aloha* (love) or fear." This clarification resonated strongly with me and seared an indelible mark in my memory.

When practicing *Olu`olu* while enhancing *Aho nui* (to be clarified in an upcoming section), we sharpen our practice of *Aloha* via developing discernment as Aunty Pilahi described, "the ability to hear what is not said, to see what cannot be seen, and to know the unknowable… from heaven's perspective, with all sides included and with the best intentions for all involved."

This blended practice embedded in developing discernment gifts us the opportunity to fully extend all our perspective antennas (traditional and nontraditional senses, including intuition) needed to see all sides… from heaven's perspective for the greatest good for all involved.

The introspection (self-reflection) connection of *Olu`olu* with *Lō kahi* is apparent when we realize that we are all spiritual/energetic human beings with bodies, hearts, and souls that need love, attention, and healing to survive and thrive. It is in this awareness of the human condition and our basic need for human connection that we begin introspection (self-reflection), which reveals the micro and macro interconnectivity of it all in the cosmos with the interconnectivity of each one of ourselves to each other, including all that exists in our world and universe.

We are all intertwined with giving and receiving assistance with our life lessons. When we practice *Olu`olu* and *Aho nui*, we are mindful of the possibility of our contamination to other people's healing processes, mindful of our fear-based tendencies and influences, while being open to inner and external guidance in each step of the process.

Olu`olu is a "deep" value that involves a vigilant practice of energetically/spiritually digging deep within us and our perceptions of our relationships with others via introspection (self-reflection), integrating our intention of *doing no harm* while being a part of our inner and external guided healing journeys.

An *Aloha* story that illustrates my perception of my *Olu`olu* practice involves one of my *aumakua*s (Hawaiian animal spiritual guides). When I shared this story with Pono, I did not recognize the connection with my *Olu`olu* practice until later during self-reflection.

STORY TIME . . .

A few years ago, my PADI scuba instructor, Kimo, and I were off the coast of Waikiki Beach completing my scuba certification training, which included a task requiring me to successfully remove, replace, and "clear" my mask three consecutive times at the bottom of the ocean floor. This task required me to exhale through my nose into my mask while gently tilting my head back with my feet on the ocean floor. Feeling comfortable and confident with this procedure from much training at the bottom of the deep end of the YMCA Kokokahi pool, I felt excited to master this procedure and move on to the next task.

During my last round of clearing my mask, Kimo was in front of me observing my progress. I looked over his shoulder and saw two small fish getting larger as they approached us. Kimo saw that my breathing had changed from slow and steady to a faster pace. He turned to see what I was looking at and then quickly encouraged me to return to my slow and steady breathing by putting his face in front of my face and breathing slowly while holding me steady and clasping my arms around my biceps.

Knowing we were too deep under the water at that point to swim to the surface quickly without serious consequences, we remained on the ocean floor while we observed the fast-approaching fish.

When the two fish started to look and appear to move like humpback whales, I signed "whale" to Kimo, and he nodded. From my perspective, one of the two whales looked considerably smaller and lighter in color than the other. The smaller one could have been a calf, making the larger one, most probably, its mother.

As they were approaching, we could hear their songs and feel the movement of the water. The mama and baby whales (as well as their songs) were beautiful! Having had a few experiences of being in the ocean and seeing humpback whales from a distance, I felt grateful and excited that my *aumakuas* (spiritual animal guides) were visiting me again. Intuitively, I knew these gentle giants would not hurt Kimo and me.

We were both facing the whales and were in awe as we observed the mama whale swim between the baby whale and us. While blowing bubbles from her blowhole, creating what appeared to me as a bubble barrier (a baby whale playpen), I felt safe. The two whales were about the distance of a school bus away from us when the mama and baby whale stopped swimming toward us. I giggled while I watched the baby whale move away from the bubble playpen and up to the surface with the mama whale.

After the whales took breaths at the water's surface, time stood still while the mama and baby lowered themselves back into the water to our level. At the time, it felt like an eternity while the whales remained in a floating position, appearing to be watching us. Imagining that I was in a different dimension (possibly a time-warp portal), I knew I was meant to be there at that place and in that moment. It felt surreal!

As the two whales started to sing again in a lower pitch, I laughed and cried at the same time, feeling joyfully tickled by this amazing experience. I believe the mama whale was singing her gentle song to keep all of us calm, to communicate with her baby, and to connect with Kimo and me.

The mama whale then turned her body to see us better, with one of her eyes looking directly at us. It felt as if she were looking into my soul! My heart felt so warm and expanded while tears of joy poured into my mask. I also felt very grateful that the mama whale trusted us. She was choosing to remain relatively close to us with her baby present. As a mama myself, I felt connected in a maternal way with the mama whale, knowing how much trust is required of a parent to have strangers around our babies. In prayer, I thanked God/LOVE/Universe for this rare experience and for this amazing visit of my *aumakuas* (spiritual animal guides). I thanked the mama whale for her love/trust by humming from my vocal cords (as well as energetically from my heart)... *Thank you!*

As the whales were swimming away, Kimo turned to me and indicated that the levels of our air tanks were low. I nodded and followed his lead as we safely returned to the water's surface and climbed back into the boat. After properly stowing our scuba equipment and removing our diving suits, we talked for a long time about our shared once-in-a-lifetime experience with the whales while drinking water, resting, and warming up in the sun.

While talking on the boat, Kimo mentioned that we spent only a few minutes with the whales during our hour in the water. It truly felt that those few minutes were a lot longer. We laughed so hard talking about our shared experience and the awe of it all that my stomach muscles hurt.

What Kimo and I both found most impressive was the gentle yet firm way the mama whale was dealing with her *kalohe* (rascal) calf (who appeared to be going rogue, related to its curiosity about us). The mama whale appeared to redirect her baby with her bubble playpen when it may have seemed to her the baby needed more than her song to change his direction. We were also both amazed with the loving energy we felt from the mama whale as she rested with her baby relatively near us. It was obvious to us that she did not feel we were a threat.

After sharing this story with Pono, I mentioned that I had previously volunteered on weekends for the Oahu-based NOAA Fisheries rescue missions, assisting distressed and/or hurt turtles, dolphins, and humpback whales. During my training for the missions, I learned a simple rescue protocol from a local *kapuna* (elder) trainer, which I include today in my daily *Olu`olu* practice. The acronym for this protocol is **PEE**. When I first heard of this protocol's acronym, I initially found it appropriate for me because one of the first things I unconsciously did underwater when I felt anxious about to assist an ocean animal, possibly in stress, was pee! The PEE protocol involved assessments of the following:

- **P**eople (the team's needs, as well as my own needs, including physical, emotional, and intuitive check-ins)
- **E**nvironment (weather, currents, water clarity, onlookers, other animals, boats, and transportation vehicles)
- **E**quipment (communication, first aid, and medical supplies for the team, the animal, as well as transportation supplies)

Following the initial assessments represented in the **PEE** protocol, I was taught to constantly keep checking with my internal and external "antennae," being open to guidance from all my sources of information. Knowing that the animal may be in pain (feeling fear), it was important for me to breathe deep belly breaths and be in the moment, open to internal and external guidance. Since my intuition is strong, I loved being with people who trusted their intuition and encouraged me to do the same.

Just like being with young children and people with communication challenges, animals cannot communicate with us using **our** verbal language. During this training process, I was encouraged to intuitively/energetically "read" the animal, my team, and the situation (utilizing all of my traditional and nontraditional senses) in my assessment, communication, and treatment assessment efforts.

When I shared this story and my evolved *Olu`olu* perspectives and practice with Pono, he said, "Good," and nodded.

HA`A HA`A

As Pilahi Paki described, the meaning of *Ha`a ha`a* is "humility to be expressed with modesty." Pono shared with me that the deeper meaning of *Ha`a ha`a* is releasing that which needs to be released (i.e., stress, anger, grieving, resentment, and other painful thoughts, emotions, and experiences) to unblock us internally and externally, as well as individually and collectively to fully be *Aloha* (love).

As I previously mentioned, during the beginning stages of my efforts in starting my Aloha Stories LLC business and while trying to self-publish my book, there was a time when I physically, mentally, emotionally, and spiritually pushed myself to learn/absorb as much as I could (and as fast as I could) to meet the needs of my growing business and book publishing efforts.

In doing so, I sacrificed my sleep routine and many other *Aka hai* self-nurturing practices, including my daily practice of *Ha`a ha`a* (going to that place of empty, releasing that which needs to be released).

Again, I had it backwards. After getting sick from exhaustion and sleep deprivation, I hit bottom with a "splat." Then I remembered at a deeper level that it is in my daily practice of the *Aloha* values, including *Ha`a ha`a,* that I quiet my mind, go to that place of empty, reconnect with my internal as well as external spiritual guides, and trust the miraculous process to unfold with and through *Aloha.*

"Emptying of myself" (or, as Pono would say, "going to that place of empty" or "going to empty") are ways of describing the daily practice of *Ha`a ha`a*. Pono also clarified that "going to the place of empty" means to energetically clean out one's internal home (inside one's heart and soul), making room for guidance and healing by removing internal emotional and spiritual blocks along the way.

As a significant part of my *Ha`a ha`a* practice, my daily journaling ritual (writing on paper and/or on my laptop) is a private, powerful, and safe way to release and process my thoughts, feelings, and stories. Later, I will then reflect on what I write, sometimes being able to connect what I write with my daily practice of *Aloha* values.

My daily *Ha`a ha`a* practice includes breath work, being in nature, meditation, walking barefoot on grass, soil and/or sand, being/swimming in the ocean, and/or going on nature hikes in the mountains, botanical gardens, and rainforests (basically being and moving in nature), along with practices of forgiveness. In the Hawaiian culture, there is an ancient forgiveness practice called *Ho`oponopono.*

Soon after my mother's passing, my family and I were blessed with a deep-rooted, ancient Hawaiian healing experience based on the *Ho`oponopono* practice (integrating aspects of self-introspection, asking for forgiveness, making amends and other components) facilitated by a well-respected local *Ho`oponopono* spiritual teacher whom Pono Shim knew personally. This spiritual teacher had been mentored by Morrnah Simeona, the Hawaiian spiritual *kahuna lapa`au* (healer) who formalized modern day *Ho`oponopono*.

Throughout the years, I have continued my practice of *Ho`oponopono* with this teacher's guidance while integrating it with the forgiveness practices based on Jesus' teachings, which I learned as a child (and continue to practice) in my Catholic (universal) faith, along with the universal spiritual teachings of love and forgiveness shared by many spiritual paths around the world such as cleansing via water (including being in the ocean) and via fire. For example, safely burning in a fireproof container such as a closed glass pot, the piece of paper my intentions for my forgiveness processes are written on.

My perspective of *Ha`a ha`a*, incorporating the practice of forgiveness, involves my acceptance of myself and others as being human... making mistakes. As I remind myself, my daughter and others, mistakes are opportunities for us to learn life's many lessons through fear or love. Our mistakes (learning opportunities) are paths of growth, not signs of weakness.

STORY TIME . . .

One particularly humbling learning opportunity I experienced while finalizing my research dissertation was that I incorrectly spelled the first name of Pono's father consistently throughout the document. During a final document spelling check effort, prior to submitting my dissertation to Argosy University, Hawaii, I accidentally changed Pono's father's first name from "Alvin" to "Albert." Albert is the first name of a distant relative of Pono, indicated on his family tree shared in my dissertation's Appendix G. By the time I discovered the error, it was too late to change it because my dissertation had already been submitted to the university and copyrighted.

When I brought this error to Pono's attention, he immediately forgave me. He asked me to share the correct spelling of his father's first name in all my subsequent *Aloha* values and *Aloha Stories* documents and all other efforts, which referred to Alvin Shim. I thanked Pono for forgiving me and humbly confirmed I would make amends by correctly stating and spelling Pono's father's first name in all my present and future references of Alvin Shim.

Pono graciously added that my daily practice of *Aloha* in their honor was more important to him than the correct spelling of anyone's name in my work. Pono then looked at me over his reading glasses and encouraged me to forgive myself for making the error. I was grateful for Pono's insight and encouragement to forgive myself, which I did in time through my practice of *Ho`oponopono.*

AHO NUI

In the humbling experience with Pono (described in the previous section), things were made right between Pono and me. Without missing a beat, Pono asked me to clarify my future intention of formally sharing the *Aloha* values and *Aloha Stories'* wisdom originally distilled in my dissertation honoring Pono, Pilahi Paki, Alvin Shim, and my childhood hula teacher, Lorraine Brandt.

STORY TIME . . .

I felt pleasantly surprised and thankful that Pono approved of my many ideas of integrating my interpretations of the *Aloha* values and my evolving *Aloha* stories into my budding Aloha Stories' education and consulting business, offering in-person and online classes and workshops, books, movies, and television series. Pono was very happy to hear my intentions of donating a portion of my business revenue to organizations I had previously volunteered with, including Aloha United Way, American Red Cross, and Give Kids the World.

In addition, Pono approved my inclusion of the United Nations to my list of beneficiaries of a portion of my book and business proceeds. I chose to add the United Nations to my list because I felt (and still feel) strongly that sharing this *Aloha* values and stories of loving/peaceful wisdom and this way of life with the world's leaders would be instrumental in promoting global peace.

In reflection, during our conversation, I can now see that Pono had been practicing *Aho nui*, which resulted in Pono "prospering" (lifting up and celebrating) me while he was practicing the integration of all the other values.

Pono's practice of *Aho nui* included acknowledging my sincerity in asking for forgiveness and my intentions of making amends (by correctly stating Pono's father's name, "Alvin Shim." His practice of *Aho nui* also involved Pono listening to the unique integrative, intuitive, and energetic perspectives and ideas, along with my creative ways of expressing the values of *Aloha*. In addition, Pono listened and celebrated my *Aloha* stories while honoring my *Aloha Stories'* mentors, including Pilahi Paki, Pono's father (Alvin Shim), my hula teacher (Lorraine Brandt), my parents, family members, ancestors, teachers, healers, and spiritual guides.

Having energetically/spiritually practiced *Aho nui* and "prospering" (lifting and celebrating) me, Pono then gently reminded me that, above all, my efforts involved in sharing the *Aloha* values through my Aloha Stories budding business are to be rooted in my daily practice of the *Aloha* values and the evolving *Aloha* stories. Pono reiterated during this closing discussion that *Aloha* (love) evolves out of our stories, and LOVE is who we all are and why we are here.

At that moment, I realized the time and told Pono I needed to leave for a previously scheduled appointment. Pono hugged me, saying, "You will know when it is time for you to do what you are meant to do. Follow your guidance and keep practicing. *Aloha*!" With a heart filled with gratitude and respect, I smiled with tears of gratitude, saying, "Mahalo! *Aloha*!"

This was the last conversation Pono and I had together prior to my work on the mainland with Delta Air Lines in Georgia and Walt Disney World in Florida. I feel deeply grateful for my mentorship with Pono Shim that catapulted me into these amazing global learning experiences which expanded my practice of the *Aloha* values and my sharing of my *Aloha* stories.

I truly believe, in the spirit of *Aho nui,* that Pono had fully opened himself to inner and external guidance prior to choosing his words and actions during our last discussion before my departure from the island. The presence of our spiritual guides and teachers "prospering" both of us during that final healing discussion was palpable.

Pono's Mix Plate — Integration of the *Aloha* Values

In addition to being a mentor, Pono was (and continues to be) a spiritual older brother for me by:

- *Olu`olu* (while doing no harm, watching out for, and guiding me)
- *Aho nui* (gently nudging me to be open to guidance and go beyond my comfort levels)
- *Lō kahi (*encouraging me to make peace with and sometimes find humor in my humanness, including my unique ways of processing/sharing energy)

I still hear Pono's heavenly big brother words of wisdom guiding me throughout my daily practice of the *Aloha* values, especially now during my writing processes involved in the manifestation of this book for you.

As a true earthly big brother, Pono was firm with me while encouraging me to push myself beyond my comfort levels, especially when I got things wrong. He was equally patient with me when I repeatedly tried to get things right in my uniquely intuitive and creative ways.

While mentoring me beyond my comfort levels, Pono "prospered" (lifted/celebrated) my daily *Aloha* values efforts with affirming subtle words (i.e., "good" and "yes"), along with equally subtle head and hand gestures, including nodding his head once and/or giving me the thumbs-up hand gesture.

Pono also celebrated my authentic *Aloha* stories with me via a full smile and sometimes laughter, especially when I started off sharing my stories feeling upside down and underwater in my sometimes-mixed-up emotions, thoughts, and words.

Pushing me beyond my comfort zone, Pono would sometimes (during my dissertation process) jokingly, in a big brother way, remind me (when he noticed I was upside down in my thoughts) to "follow the bubbles," which is how a surfer finds their way back to the surface of the water (to breathe) after experiencing a major wipeout.

Pono encouraged me when I found myself in symbolic deep and turbulent water to follow the direction of the surface floating bubbles (internal and external guidance) in the water (in life) as I was trying to find my way up to the water's surface (the truth or essence of what I found myself upside down in) to breathe freely, physically and spiritually once again.

In other words, "follow the bubbles" translated to me to mean that I needed to practice *Aho nui* the way I dealt with a surfing wipeout by being still, relaxing, being patient, and being perceptive (of guidance). This was (and still is) a very challenging practice for me.

Many times, when finding myself in the midst of fear-based turbulent waters, I hear Pono's encouraging words as I feel upside down in my thoughts to "follow the bubbles" and find my way up to the surface (air) breathing in my truth, which is always *Aloha* (love). In time, as I continue to practice *Aho nui*, life's "turbulence" subsides.

Yes, I feel Pono nudging me in a spiritual big brother way to "follow the bubbles" when I experience emotionally turbulent life wipeouts. I smile when I hear his words in my head/heart reminding me to intuitively ride my guidance-led waves to shore by practicing *Aloha* (love) in all things, including writing this book and growing my Aloha Stories LLC business.

STORY TIME . . .

While Pono and I were waiting outside of an Argosy University conference room to begin one of my formal dissertation-related interviews with him, out of the blue, Pono metaphorically turned the tables on me and started to ask me questions about my `Ōlelo Community Television producer experiences involved with my (at the time two years running) weekly television series called, *Portuguese in Hawaii* featuring Hawaii's Portuguese living legend, Herb Carlos (one of my mother's and my Portuguese storytelling mentors).

In previous decades, Herb had shared his perspectives of Portuguese history, language, culture, music, art, and genealogy, integrated with his personal stories for the people of Hawaii through his weekly Hawaii public radio show.

Pono started his inquiry by asking me how it all started. I simply responded by saying I was gifted the opportunity to be molded in the processes of photography and video production from a child throughout my young adult life by my mother's father, Grandpa (George Cabral Sr.), who was a professional Hawaii Advertiser Newspaper lead photographer and local television news station legendary lead cameraman/videographer.

Grandpa was known for telling amazing stories through his photos and videos. It was in his darkroom (which he constructed in his garage), on his picnic table, and at his kitchen table that Grandpa shared his stories with me of his wisdom, knowledge, and expertise related to his practice of *Aloha* (love) that evolved into his wonderful stories, captured in photos and video, as well as his own voice.

I continued sharing with Pono my divinely guided experience of being mentored by `Ōlelo Community Television (Hawaii Public Video Production) team members through their multitude of layers of training, particularly with the Waipahu Center's team director and gifted staff (some of whom previously worked with my Grandpa Cabral). Through hard work and a series of miraculous events, I became the producer of a co-created weekly television series called *Portuguese in Hawaii* featuring Herb Carlos.

Herb had been recently diagnosed with cancer and approached me at a local Portuguese *festa* (festival), having heard from a family member that I was training to be an `Ōlelo producer. He asked me to help him share his stories about the Portuguese in Hawaii via a weekly television series. I said yes, and our adventure began.

Pono laughed as I shared with him my many stories about being a new producer on a shoestring budget (basically having no money to do what needed to be done) for this noble production. As my mother told me, "Necessity is the mother of innovation." In other words, needing certain things for the production, I became very resourceful with what was available on set (three artificial trees, a table, two chairs, bricks, rocks, boxes, milk crates, and the technical video and audio equipment).

All of this was enhanced by items I borrowed from my family, my home, and the Portuguese community (including blankets, tablecloths, costume and clothing items, food, books, musical instruments, pieces of art, nautical instruments, and other props). I was flying by the seat of my pants during this highly exciting and fulfilling experience.

Yes, a miraculously glorious television program was born in the midst of many challenges. When I look back on those experiences and my conversation of these experiences with Pono, I now can see that Pono was "prospering" (lifting and celebrating) me and my experience in celebrating the gems of wisdom I gleaned from that transformational journey with Herb Carlos.

As my doctorate-level dissertation process, in addition to my full-time job at the university, became more demanding (providing less time for me to focus on the production of the series), my `Ōlelo mentor and his team greatly assisted in helping me continue the series production for a few more years, up to Herb's passing.

Pono mentioned that the experience spiritually fed all involved. I wholeheartedly agreed! The production team and I individually and collectively felt excited and grateful to be a part of this parting gift from, through, and for Herb Carlos, benefiting Herb, our team, Herb's family, and the people of Hawaii for generations to come.

A few years ago, under the director of the Waipahu `Ōlelo Studio's guidance, Herb's family was gifted a complete set of the television series prior to `Ōlelo unfortunately needing to delete their copy of the series in its entirety from its overfull database, to make room for new `Ōlelo television series and productions.

I cherish my memories of that unique experience and thanked Pono for listening to and celebrating these life-enhancing experiences with me. I remember telling Pono that I felt (and still feel) more alive being involved in video storytelling (i.e., movie and TV series productions) than writing storytelling projects because I thought (and still think) in multi-dimensional and multi-sensory (Star Trek holodeck-like) projections.

Being involved in video storytelling projects reminded me of how I felt as a third grader, thoroughly enjoying the process of creating, directing, producing mini skits, plays, and video projects for my class. Pono shifted his weight slightly, leaned his head to one side, and in deep thought, said, "Huh."

At that time, Pono revealed to me that he had watched a few of my *Portuguese in Hawaii* early episodes, including one of the first episodes when I was interviewing the English-speaking Portuguese sailing crew members on their spotless and sparkling clean Portuguese sailing vessel. They had just docked that morning in Honolulu Harbor near Aloha Tower after sailing from Lisbon, Portugal, to Honolulu. Unfortunately, Herb was not well enough to join me for that day's shoot. Consequently, once again, I was flying by the seat of my pants during that production. Fortunately, I had done my research and had a list of interview questions prepared for this unique event.

Pono started to laugh remembering a portion of that episode. At first, I did not think it was funny at all because it involved a wide-brimmed hat I had bought for the event, which I almost lost. It was a very windy day, and this beautiful hat flew off my head while I was in the middle of asking the boat captain a few questions during our one small window of time allotted to video this part of the experience because the captain needed to attend to another matter.

As we were walking to a higher level of the boat, the captain was slipped a note. He discreetly shared with me off camera (while the camera crew was scanning to the horizon to highlight the gorgeous harbor view) that he only had a couple of minutes for the shoot because of a pressing matter due to the wind picking up.

According to Pono, during his viewing of the episode, the captain's eyes looked like they popped out of his head as I continued asking him a question while I grabbed my hat by the outer brim mid-flight off of my head (with my hair all *kapakahi* (mixed-up) blowing in the breeze), returned the hat back to my head, and kept my hand on the hat during the continued gusts of wind, without missing a beat during the interview, while smiling.

At this point, I interrupted Pono by explaining that the camera crew had almost dropped their equipment due to the strong gusts of wind, and I was multitasking! While bracing the bottom of the tripod, holding the camera with my foot to stabilize it while holding the microphone in one hand, catching the hat with the other hand, I was preparing to drop everything to catch the camera if it started to fall in my direction.

After bursting out in laughter, Pono said I looked like the flying nun getting ready to take flight. I was familiar with the popular TV series *The Flying Nun* starring Sally Fields. While Pono kept laughing, I stopped to think about what he had just said and wondered how it connected to my *Aloha* practice.

Not knowing how to take all of this, I first frowned, then looked confused, and then half smiled to give the impression that I thought it was funny and said, "Thank you," which caused Pono to laugh harder. I did not know what else to say while Pono kept laughing. At the time, I did not fully get what he was describing until I went back and reviewed the episode. With Pono's descriptions in mind while revisiting the scene on video, I laughed my *okole* (bottom) off. It was funny!

I found irony in this current situation of Pono interviewing me while we were waiting for the conference room to become available for me to interview Pono. In essence, who was the interviewer and who was the interviewee?

While waiting, Pono continued asking me questions about the *Portuguese in Hawaii* television series production. In response to Pono's question about how much time was involved in my writing of each episode's script, I laughed and said, "What script?" Herb just needed me to ask him a few questions on the topic he wanted to focus on during the videoing of the episode and join in conversation with him as he shared his wisdom through his stories.

My job as the producer was to get everything lined up with the production preparation so that when Herb arrived, he would share his storyboard-ish outline of the episode with me, highlighting what he wanted to focus on in the order he wanted the topics to flow. We then discussed bullet points of how we would navigate through the shoot with me giving broad-stroke directions to the production crew.

Then it was game on…we just rolled with it. It was fun! Biology breaks were taken when needed. For the most part, the episodes were recorded in one continuous shot, and then the editing work began. Again, the production team had magical powers and did the heavy lifting behind the camera and in editing to make the series such a success. Herb was the star who captured everyone's hearts, souls, and minds with his amazing perspectives, love, humor, and stories.

Pono wanted more details, so I explained basically how a shoot would roll. Herb walked in with his outline for the show written on a piece of paper that he barely referred to during the shoot. From his rich life and his seasoned weekly radio station experiences, Herb just spoke from the heart and what evolved out of him was spectacular.

When I was in the interviewer role of the shoots, I just winged it! I knew Herb for years through my mother and grandparents as well as my personal experience with Herb via my family's involvement with a local Portuguese dance troop my mother helped organize, along with the Hawaii Council on Portuguese Heritage my parents led for years. Herb was also instrumental in mentoring my mother for the Hawaii Portuguese Heritage Family Summer Camps she created and orchestrated.

Herb was like an uncle to me, as well as my mother's and now my mentor. It was fun being around Herb! You never knew what he was going to say. Like Grandpa Cabral, Herb's Portuguese jokes and stories brought humor to the human condition (not poking fun at the Portuguese culture). From my perspective, similar to Pono, Herb lived his life being *Aloha* and "prospering" (lifting and celebrating) each person he met while being an amazing storyteller.

I told Pono that there were times in the production shoots when it felt like there was a room full of heavenly angels supporting all of us while we were supporting Herb during his magnificently self-designed swan song television episodes.

When Herb was getting closer to his spiritual transition, he insisted on showing up for the shoots with a water bottle, his pain medicine, and the shoot's highlight notes. My Waipahu Center mentor, especially at this time, did the heavy lifting of shooting and editing these final productions while I was busy wrapping up my research dissertation.

Herb's perseverance and unique sense of humor kept the team going. Herb was on a mission! With divine guidance and support, Herb was able to see it through to its completion. We were gifted time to create a pot-luck celebration for Herb at the studio before his passing, including the `Ōlelo team involved in the production and his family. It was truly a glorious life celebration!

Pono smiled when I was done sharing about Herb and the *Portuguese in Hawaii* television series. Pono then nodded and said, "Good," as we entered the conference room, where I began my interview of Pono for my dissertation process.

Pono was fascinated with my stories about Herb Carlos and my *Portuguese in Hawaii* television series story. From time to time, Pono asked me to tell him more of these stories. In reflection, I can now see how in many ways, there are parallels between Pono, Herb, and many other legendary storytellers I have been blessed to be mentored by over the years.

These storytellers (like other significant storytellers of their timeless evolved level) shared their life wisdom through stories — not generated from their minds but rather from their hearts, souls, and authentic life experiences. The stories poured out of them from their way of being *Aloha*, of their own unique perspectives of life and love, as well as their ways of connecting with their Higher Power/Universe, themselves, and others.

It was a bittersweet experience preparing to leave Hawaii after I completed my research dissertation experience, ending my doctorate degree journey. I felt grateful for the transformative experiences with my family, my Argosy *ohana*, my `Ōlelo family (including Herb), Pono, and all my other loving earthly angels during this part of my journey. I also knew I would greatly miss being around these supportive people while I lived for a short time off the island.

When I left Oahu a few days after saying *Mahalo* and *Aloha* to Pono and my family, I began my new adventure in Florida, working for Walt Disney World in their College and Internship Program. There, I was guided to additional earthly angels/mentors, including Kaui Mahikoa Brandt (also known as Aunty Kaui), who happened to be related by marriage to my childhood hula teacher, Lorraine Brandt. That divinely guidance family connection of Lorraine Brandt with Aunty Kaui blew me away!

Aunty Kaui also knew of Pono Shim, Pilahi Paki, Alvin Shim, and their Aloha Ambassador work on Oahu. Aunty Kaui and I enjoyed talking about our daily practices of the values of *Aloha* while "talking story." She took me under her wing, and I felt "prospered" by her as a welcomed member of her *ohana* (family).

Aunty Kaui mentored thousands of people from the Polynesian Islands via her leadership role at the Walt Disney World Polynesian Village Resort. I felt honored to be mentored by her during my time with Disney. I cherish my wonderful memories with Aunty Kaui, talking about our families, Hawaii, our practices of the *Aloha* values, and dancing hula together. Being with Aunty Kaui so far away from home felt like being with my family! She was *ohana*!

Aunty Kaui introduced me to my amazing Disney Institute mentor, who guided me in creating my first professional team building and leadership training projects integrated with *Aloha.*

Throughout my experiences with Walt Disney World, Delta Air Lines, and subsequent education intertwined with consulting professional experiences, I continued to practice what I learned from Pono, enhanced by Aunty Kaui and my other Aloha Ambassador mentors, related to the *Aloha* values and sharing with others my *Aloha* stories in my voice, as well as my unique ways of being.

A few years ago, my fiancé (now husband) and I visited Pono at his Honolulu office prior to Granny Cabral's life celebration following her passing. This was the first time Pono met my fiancé. Pono greeted both of us with warm *Aloha* hugs! We enjoyed "talking story" with Pono. It was wonderful catching up and "prospering" (lifting and celebrating) each other. I feel grateful I had the opportunity to thank Pono in person for continuing to be my mentor and my spiritual big brother one last time before his passing.

Yes, I still feel Pono's mentorship and spiritual, big brotherly ways of guiding me today. I sense Pono is continuing to watch over me from heaven, nudging me to be my unique creative self (with my unique perspectives of the *Aloha* values and *Aloha* stories), going to that place of empty beyond my comfort levels, as well as laughing humbly at my humanness.

I pray what I have expressed in this book resonates with you and assists you on your journey, just as Pono's mentorship, enhanced by his big brother ways, continues to assist me in moving me forward in my efforts of sharing *Aloha* values and *Aloha* stories. With deep respect and gratitude, I share these treasured stories of *Aloha* with you in honor of Pono.

Thanks to Pono and my other Aloha Ambassador mentors/angels, while practicing *Aloha* daily, I believe that I am becoming more aware of the deeper meanings of the values of *Aloha* in real time… in the present moment. In particular, my practice of *Aho nui* (which I perceive to involve being patient in the stillness, observing internal and external guidance, and waiting for the moment to respond rather than react with love) is improving.

When I take time daily to practice *Ha`a ha`a,* including being still (going to that place of empty and, at times, including self-reflection and forgiveness), I am gifted with a deeper awareness of who I am along with why I am here (in relationship to myself, others and all that exists).

To recap, there is no one way of practicing any of the *Aloha* values or one way of sharing *Aloha* stories. The *Aloha* values are not meant to be practiced by themselves. They are meant to be practiced together like musical instruments in a symphony harmonizing with each other, just as *Aloha* stories are meant to be shared with others as they authentically emerge from our hearts/souls and daily practice.

My attention to the aspects of my daily practice of the *Aloha* values changes day to day depending on what is going on internally and externally. The one constant thing is Pono's voice in my head and heart, reminding me to let go with my head and open my heart to the values of *Aloha.*

The major "work" for me currently is being gentle and kind with myself (*Aka hai*) and taking time daily for my *Ha`a ha`a* practice of being quiet/still, going to that place of empty integrating introspection (self-reflection) in my practice of *Olu`olu* within myself and with others. When I do honor my daily practice of the *Aloha* values (including *Aka hai*, *Lō kahi, Olu`olu*, *Ha`a ha`a* and *Aho nui*), my day flows smoothly with effortless guidance, which helps me feel more relaxed, joyful, and harmonious within myself as well as with others.

Sharing our *Aloha* stories is a way of life, a practice, and a universal, spiritual/energetic process that requires patience and harmonious integration of our (individual, as well as collective) evolving perceptions along with our daily practice of the *Aloha* values.

Inner and global peace is possible through our daily practice of the *Aloha* values, which evolves into sharing our authentic *Aloha* stories with each other. Join me in this individual, local, and global effort to peacefully transform ourselves and our world through *Aloha.*

Carole's Evolving Perceptions

My assimilated perception of the *Aloha* values (which evolved to our *Aloha* stories and are based on Pilahi Paki's originally formulated *Aloha* values) is intended to honor the wisdom shared with me by/through my mentors, along with my spiritual teachers/guides including Pono Shim, Alvin Shim, Pilahi Paki, Lorraine Brandt, and Kauihealani Brandt. As Pono clarified, the *Aloha* values are to be practiced within oneself, with others, and with all that exists.

Pilahi Paki's original values of *Aloha* are:

Aka hai means **kindness**, to be expressed with **tenderness**
Lō kahi means **unity**, to be expressed with **harmony**
Olu`olu means **agreeable**, to be expressed with **pleasantness**
Ha`a ha`a means **humility**, to be expressed with **modesty**
Aho nui means **patience**, to be expressed with **perseverance**

My assimilated perspective of the *Aloha* values is the internal and external practices of:

Aka hai: being **kind** showing **tenderness** (as one loves an innocent newborn baby)
Lō kahi: being **harmonious** galvanizing peaceful **unity** (aware that we were, are and will forever be LOVE/energy connected…never broken)

Olu`olu: being **agreeable** demonstrating **pleasantness**
(“prospering” lifting/celebrating ourselves and
others while doing no harm)
Ha`a ha`a: being **humble** and **modest**
(going to the place of empty, which opens windows
to self-reflection and forgiveness)
Aho nui: being **patient** in my **perseverance**
(opening up to inner and external guidance prior to
moving forward in loving action)

In a nutshell, our *Aloha* stories evolve from our individual and collective daily practices of the *Aloha* values. The *Aloha* values interwoven with *Aloha* stories connect and “prosper” (lift/celebrate) us internally, locally, and globally.

Reflected in my unique voice, facial expressions, body language, sign language, and hand gestures (available through a free complimentary series of video clips found on www.AlohaStories.org), I open-heartedly share my evolving perspectives of the *Aloha* values and *Aloha* stories with you.

May this distillment of wisdom be helpful for all of us while we harmoniously co-create a peaceful world NOW and for future generations, one day at a time.

Please be sure to visit www.AlohaStories.org for additional information related to my evolving perceptions and practices of the *Aloha* values and *Aloha* stories.

Conclusion

Our *Aloha* stories innately emerge from our daily practice of *Aloha*. Sharing our *Aloha* stories with other people assists us in recognizing the *Aloha* (love) we see within ourselves and each other. Sharing our *Aloha* stories with others harmoniously connects us to our fellow spiritual human *ohana* (family) via our shared human experiences. It is that simple and that profound!

Mahalo nui loa for gifting me the opportunity to share (in my unique voice and creative expressions) my evolving assimilated perception of the *Aloha* values and *Aloha* stories with you, honoring the gems of wisdom and *Aloha* my mentor Pono Shim and other Aloha Ambassador mentors (as well as spiritual guides) have shared with me.

May we individually and collectively remember who we are (love) and why we are here (to share our love) while we share our *Aloha* stories (which evolve from our daily practice of *Aloha*) with each other. May we BE the *ALOHA* and PEACE we wish to see in the world!

Based on the eternal heartfelt Hawaiian and English words written in 1878 by Queen *Liliuokalani* (Hawaii's only queen regent and last sovereign monarch), I conclude this part of my journey together with YOU (the reader) with the first part of the chorus in the Queen's love song, "Aloha `Oe."

Aloha `oe, aloha `oe
E ke onaona noho i ka lipo
One fond embrace,
A ho`i a`e au
Until we meet again

English Translation:

Farewell to thee [you], farewell to thee [you]
The charming one who dwells in the shaded bowers [shade]
One fond embrace [hug],
`Ere [Before] I depart
Until we meet again

About the Author

Dr. Carole Aloha Hope Lockard is an intuitive, creative, and joyful Ambassador of Aloha. Carole shares her *Aloha* (love) through her *Aloha* stories (promoting inner and global love, peace, and joy).

Having been born and raised in a large Portuguese family (rooted in Hawaii for many generations), Carole continues to be immersed in the Hawaiian culture's harmonious rhythm overflowing with *Aloha*, which embraces and transforms people in the Islands as well as around the world.

Throughout the years, Carole has been strongly influenced by the *Aloha* values (publicly formalized by Pilahi Paki), shared with Carole when she was a young girl by her hula teacher, and then later as an adult enhanced by her Aloha Ambassador mentor, Pono Shim (via a doctorate research study).

Pono galvanized Carole's growing understanding and practice of the *Aloha* values, interwoven with his practice of storytelling... from heaven's perspective.

Aloha Stories LLC
Evolving Services and Products include:

- **Aloha Values Introduction Video Series**
  Complimentary via www.AlohaStories.org

- **Aloha Stories Education**
  Coaching, Classes, Workshops and Seminars
  Aloha Stories Book Series (starting with this book)
  Future Movies and Television Series

- **Organizational Leadership Consultation**
  Leadership Training
  Team Building

- **Aloha Stories Research Dissertation**
  Complimentary via www.AlohaStories.org

Visit www.AlohaStories.org for more information and updates.

Made in the USA
Las Vegas, NV
26 January 2024